TYPE 2 DIABETES

Cookbook for Beginners 2024

2000 | Days of Type 2 Diabetes Recipes with a Carefully Crafted 28-Day Meal Plan to Control Your Blood Sugar, Transform Your Diet and Health

Imogen Cox

EASILY CONTROL YOUR BLOOD SUGAR EVERY DAY

2,000 DAYS OF QUICK, EASY, LOW-SUGAR RECIPES AND 28 DAYS OF MEAL PLANS

STEP-BY-STEP INSTRUCTIONS
NUTRITIONAL ANALYSIS
EACH MEAL FOR WORRY-FREE EATING

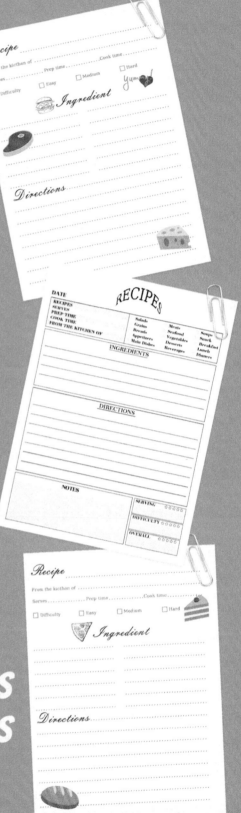

CONTENTS

INTRODUCTION.................................6

What do you know about Diabetes? 7

Foods Diabetics should eat and avoid......................7

How can this Diabetics Cookbook help you? 8

Measurement Conversions...............**10**

28–Day Meal Plan **12**

Breakfast Recipes **14**

Fresh Fruit Combo 16

Apple Spiced Tea 16

Raspberry Peach Puff Pancake...........................16

Calico Scrambled Eggs 17

Mixed Fruit With Lemon-basil Dressing 17

Maple Apple Baked Oatmeal 18

Guacamole 18

Appetizers And Snacks **19**

Cheesy Snack Mix 21

Pickled Shrimp With Basil..................................21

Lime'd Blueberries 21

Garden-fresh Wraps 22

Tomato-jalapeno Granita 22

Crostini With Kalamata Tomato 22

Mango Avocado Spring Rolls 23

Balsamic-goat Cheese Grilled Plums....................23

Asian Marinated Mushrooms...............................23

Fish & Seafood Recipes **24**

Tomato-poached Halibut...................................26

Crunchy Tuna Wraps..26

Fantastic Fish Tacos 27

Cheesy Shrimp And Grits 27

Creamy Chipotle Chile Sauce 28

Seared Scallops With Snap Pea And Edamame Slaw....28

Potatoes, Pasta, And Whole Grains..**29**

Chickpeas With Garlic And Parsley...........................31

Sicilian White Beans And Escarole 31

Warm Farro With Mushrooms And Thyme 32

Wheat Berry Salad With Roasted Red Pepper, Feta, And Arugula 32

Brown Rice With Tomatoes And Chickpeas..................33

Parmesan Potato Bake......................................33

Vegetarian Recipes...........................**34**

Light Parmesan Pasta 36

Avocado & Garbanzo Bean Quinoa Salad...................36

Tomato Topper Over Anything 36

Ricotta-stuffed Portobello Mushrooms 37

Tasty Lentil Tacos 37

Black Beans With Bell Peppers & Rice 38

Skillet-grilled Meatless Burgers With Spicy Sour Cream 38

Salads Recipes **39**

Edamame Corn Carrot Salad 41

Warm Spinach Salad With Feta And Pistachios............41

Cumin'd Salsa Salad 41

Lemony Asparagus Spear Salad.............................42

Gazpacho Salad...42

Chunky Veggie Slaw...42

Meat Recipes.................................43

Weeknight Pasta...45

Greek-style Ravioli..45

Open-faced Roast Beef Sandwiches 45

Smoky Sirloin 46

Garlic Pork Roast..46

One-pot Beef & Pepper Stew...............................47

Sassy Salsa Meat Loaves 47

Soups, Stews, And Chilis...............48

Italian Veggie Beef Soup....................................50

Creamy Butternut Soup......................................50

Chinese Starter Soup...50

Hearty Vegetable Lentil Soup 51

Sausage & Greens Soup.....................................51

Chicken Tortilla Soup With Greens 52

Cold-day Chicken Noodle Soup 52

Poultry Recipes 53

Sausage-topped White Pizza...............................55

Spicy Barbecued Chicken...................................55

Citrus-spiced Roast Chicken...............................56

Balsamic Chicken With Roasted Tomatoes 56

Cool & Crunchy Chicken Salad...........................56

Slow Cooker Favorites.....................57

Braised Swiss Chard With Shiitakes And Peanuts.........59

Chicken Thighs With Black-eyed Pea Ragout 59

Teriyaki Beef Stew...60

And Radishes 60

Carne Guisada...61

Spiced Pork Tenderloin With Carrots Slow Cooker Beef Tostadas...61

Special Treats 62

Fig Bars...64

Saucy Spiced Pears 64

Frozen Yogurt Fruit Pops 65

Peaches, Blackberries, And Strawberries With Basil And Pepper 65

No-fuss Banana Ice Cream 65

Nectarines And Berries In Prosecco 66

Strawberry Pot Stickers.....................................66

Vegetables, Fruit And Side Dishes ...67

Squash Melt 69

Smoky Cauliflower 69

Fresh Lemon Roasted Brussels Sprouts.................69

Roasted Beans And Green Onions 70

Parmesan Butternut Squash 70

Confetti Corn 70

Sautéed Zucchini Ribbons 71

Hot Skillet Pineapple 71

Appendix : Recipes Index..................72

INTRODUCTION

Imogen Cox, a renowned nutritionist and passionate advocate for balanced, health-conscious eating, brings his wealth of expertise to the forefront of this remarkable cookbook. With a deep understanding of the unique needs of those living with diabetes, he has crafted a collection of recipes that not only adhere to strict nutritional guidelines but also tantalize the taste buds with a rich tapestry of flavors, textures, and colors. Through his work, Cox not only provides a lifeline for those managing diabetes but also empowers them to embrace a lifestyle that's not just about restrictions but about the joy of savoring every bite.

Diagnosed with diabetes himself, Imogen Cox understands the challenges of navigating this condition firsthand. His personal journey, coupled with his extensive professional experience, has led him to create a cookbook that is much more than a mere collection of recipes; it is a comprehensive guide to living well with diabetes. With a mission to shatter the myth that diabetic meals are dull and monotonous, Cox introduces readers to a vibrant and delectable world where food becomes a source of nourishment, pleasure, and empowerment.

Cox's Diabetic Cookbook is a beacon of hope for those striving to manage their diabetes effectively, as it navigates the intricate nuances of the condition with grace and finesse. With a focus on whole, unprocessed foods, balanced macronutrients, and portion control, this cookbook equips individuals with the tools they need to maintain stable blood sugar levels, control their weight, and safeguard their heart health. It's a testament to the fact that, with the right guidance and a dash of culinary creativity, living with diabetes can be an exquisite gastronomic adventure.

In this cookbook, Imogen Cox unveils a treasure trove of recipes that encompass the entire spectrum of culinary experiences. From hearty breakfasts that kickstart your day on the right note to elegant dinners that turn every meal into a celebration, his cookbook covers it all. Each recipe is meticulously crafted, not only to meet the dietary requirements of individuals with diabetes but also to deliver a feast for the senses. Cox's culinary artistry shines through in his ability to marry the principles of healthy eating with an explosion of flavors and textures that dance harmoniously on the palate.

As you embark on this culinary adventure with Imogen Cox, you'll discover that his Diabetic Cookbook is not just a collection of recipes; it's a roadmap to a healthier, more vibrant life. It's a testament to the fact that, with the right knowledge, tools, and an unwavering commitment to your well-being, you can not only manage diabetes effectively but also relish every delicious bite along the way. Imogen Cox's passion for health, his personal journey, and his culinary artistry come together in this cookbook to inspire and empower individuals living with diabetes to savor the richness of life, one mouthwatering dish at a time.

What do you know about Diabetes?

Diabetes is a chronic disease characterized by persistently high levels of glucose (sugar) in the blood. The body's ability to regulate blood sugar is usually impaired due to insufficient insulin production, reduced sensitivity to insulin, or both. There are several types of diabetes, the most common being Type 1 and Type 2.

● **Type 1 Diabetes**

This autoimmune disease usually develops in childhood or adolescence. It occurs when the immune system mistakenly attacks and destroys insulin-producing cells in the pancreas. people with type 1 diabetes require a lifetime of insulin to regulate their blood glucose levels.

● **Type 2 Diabetes**

This is the most common form of diabetes and is usually associated with a lifestyle of poor diet, obesity, and lack of exercise. the body of a person with type 2 diabetes becomes resistant to the effects of insulin, and the pancreas may not be able to produce enough insulin to maintain normal blood glucose levels. the pancreas may not be able to produce enough insulin to maintain normal blood glucose levels. Treatment usually involves dietary changes, exercise, oral medications, and in some cases insulin.

In addition, gestational diabetes occurs during pregnancy when the body is unable to produce enough insulin to meet the increased demand, resulting in high blood sugar. It usually resolves after delivery, but increases the risk of developing type 2 diabetes later in life.

Common symptoms of diabetes include excessive thirst, frequent urination, unexplained weight loss, fatigue, blurred vision and slow wound healing. Uncontrolled diabetes over a long period of time can lead to serious complications, including heart disease, stroke, kidney disease, neuropathy, eye disease and circulatory problems.

Controlling diabetes requires lifestyle changes and sometimes medication or insulin therapy. This includes monitoring blood glucose levels, eating a balanced diet, engaging in regular physical activity, and taking medications as prescribed. Maintaining a healthy lifestyle is essential to preventing or controlling diabetes and reducing the risk of complications.

Foods Diabetics should eat and avoid

Foods to Eat

Non-starchy vegetables: leafy greens, broccoli, cauliflower and bell peppers

Whole grains: choose whole grains such as quinoa, brown rice and whole grain breads

Lean proteins: skinless poultry, fish, lean beef or lean pork, tofu and beans

Healthy fats: avocados, nuts, seeds and olive oil

Fruits in moderation: choose lower sugar fruits such as berries, cherries and apples

Low-fat dairy products: Choose low-fat or skim dairy products to limit saturated fat intake.

Beans and legumes: rich in fiber and protein, low on the glycemic index

Foods to avoid or limit

Sugar-sweetened beverages: avoid sugary sodas, fruit juices and energy drinks

Refined carbohydrates: eat less food made with white flour, such as white bread and sugary cereals

Processed snacks: eat fewer highly processed sugary snacks such as cookies, candies and pastries.

Saturated and trans fats: fried foods, fatty meats and commercial baked goods.

Excessive salt: limit high-sodium foods and be careful with canned and processed foods.

Excessive portion sizes: Portion control is important. Excessive consumption of healthy foods can also affect blood sugar.

Hidden sugars: such as salad dressings, sauces and condiments.

How can this Diabetics Cookbook help you?

BLOOD SUGAR CONTROL

A well-designed diabetes cookbook provides recipes that are mindful of carbohydrate content, portion sizes, and the glycemic index. This helps regulate blood sugar levels, preventing sharp spikes and crashes.

HEALTHY EATING HABITS

These cookbooks encourage balanced and nutritious eating habits, which are essential for individuals with diabetes. They promote whole foods, non-starchy vegetables, lean proteins, and whole grains, fostering a balanced diet.

WEIGHT MANAGEMENT

Maintaining a healthy weight is crucial for diabetes management. Many diabetes cookbooks offer recipes that support weight loss or maintenance, which is essential for blood sugar control.

HEART HEALTH

Diabetes is often associated with an increased risk of heart disease. Diabetes cookbooks typically emphasize heart-healthy ingredients and cooking methods, such as using healthy fats and reducing sodium.

DIVERSE AND FLAVORFUL MEALS

A diabetes cookbook can prove that eating healthily doesn't mean sacrificing flavor. It offers a wide variety of tasty recipes, dispelling the notion that diabetes-friendly meals are bland or restrictive.

PORTION CONTROL

These cookbooks often include recommended portion sizes, which is crucial for individuals with diabetes to prevent overeating and manage their carbohydrate intake effectively.

MEAL PLANNING

Diabetes cookbooks may offer meal plans and ideas, making it easier to plan balanced meals and snacks. This can simplify the often overwhelming task of meal planning.

IMPROVED NUTRITION AWARENESS

Reading and using a diabetes cookbook can increase your knowledge about nutrition and the impact of different foods on blood sugar. This knowledge can empower you to make informed food choices.

Measurement Conversions

BASIC KITCHEN CONVERSIONS & EQUIVALENT

DRY MEASUREMENTS CONVERSION CHART

3 TEASPOONS = 1 TABLESPOON = 1/16 CUP

6 TEASPOONS = 2 TABLESPOONS = 1/8 CUP

12 TEASPOONS = 4 TABLESPOONS = 1/4 CUP

24 TEASPOONS = 8 TABLESPOONS = 1/2 CUP

36 TEASPOONS = 12 TABLESPOONS = 3/4 CUP

48 TEASPOONS = 16 TABLESPOONS = 1 CUP

METRIC TO US COOKING CONVERSIONS

OVEN TEMPERATURE

120°C = 250° F

160°C = 320° F

180°C = 350° F

205°C = 400° F

220°C = 425° F

OVEN TEMPERATURE

8 FLUID OUNCES = 1 CUP = 1/2 PINT = 1/4 QUART

16 FLUID OUNCES = 2 CUPS = 1 PINT = 1/2 QUART

32 FLUID OUNCES = 4 CUPS = 2 PINTS = 1 QUART = 1/4 GALLON

128 FLUID OUNCES = 16 CUPS = 8 PINTS = 4 QUARTS = 1 GALLON

BAKING IN GRAMS

1 CUP FLOUR = 140 GRAMS

1 CUP SUGAR = 150 GRAMS

1 CUP POWDERED SUGAR = 160 GRAMS

1 CUP HEAVY CREAM = 235 GRAMS

VOLUME

1 MILLILITER = 1/5 TEASPOON

5 ML = 1 TEASPOON

15 ML = 1 TABLESPOON

240 ML = 1 CUP OR 8 FLUID OUNCES

1 LITER = 34 FL. OUNCES

WEIGHT

1 GRAM = .035 OUNCES

100 GRAMS = 3.5 OUNCES

500 GRAMS = 1.1 POUNDS

1 KILOGRAM = 35 OUNCES

US TO METRIC COOKING CONVERSIONS

1/5 TSP = 1 ML

1 TSP = 5 ML

1 TBSP = 15 ML

1 FL OUNCE = 30 ML

1 CUP = 237 ML

1 PINT (2 CUPS) = 473 ML

1 QUART (4 CUPS) = .95 LITER

1 GALLON (16 CUPS) = 3.8 LITERS

1 OZ = 28 GRAMS

1 POUND = 454 GRAMS

BUTTER

1 CUP BUTTER = 2 STICKS = 8 OUNCES = 230 GRAMS = 8 TABLESPOONS

BUTTER

1 CUP = 8 FLUID OUNCES

1 CUP = 16 TABLESPOONS

1 CUP = 48 TEASPOONS

1 CUP = 1/2 PINT

1 CUP = 1/4 QUART

1 CUP = 1/16 GALLON

1 CUP = 240 ML

BAKING PAN CONVERSIONS

1 CUP ALL-PURPOSE FLOUR = 4.5 OZ

1 CUP ROLLED OATS = 3 OZ 1 LARGE EGG = 1.7 OZ

1 CUP BUTTER = 8 OZ

1 CUP MILK = 8 OZ

1 CUP HEAVY CREAM = 8.4 OZ

1 CUP GRANULATED SUGAR = 7.1 OZ

1 CUP PACKED BROWN SUGAR = 7.75 OZ

1 CUP VEGETABLE OIL = 7.7 OZ

1 CUP UNSIFTED POWDERED SUGAR = 4.4 OZ

BAKING PAN CONVERSIONS

9-INCH ROUND CAKE PAN = 12 CUPS

10-INCH TUBE PAN =16 CUPS

11-INCH BUNDT PAN = 12 CUPS

9-INCH SPRINGFORM PAN = 10 CUPS

9 X 5 INCH LOAF PAN = 8 CUPS

9-INCH SQUARE PAN = 8 CUPS

28-Day Meal Plan

DAY	Breakfast	Lunch	Dinner
1	Apple Spiced Tea 16	Garden-fresh Wraps 22	Peaches, Blackberries, And Strawberries With Basil And Pepper 65
2	Calico Scrambled Eggs 17	Saucy Spiced Pears 64	Mango Avocado Spring Rolls 23
3	Mixed Fruit With Lemon-basil Dressing 17	Warm Farro With Mushrooms And Thyme 32	Tomato-poached Halibut 26
4	Cheesy Snack Mix 21	Ricotta-stuffed Portobello Mushroom 37	Fantastic Fish Tacos 27
5	Pickled Shrimp With Basil 21	Edamame Corn Carrot Salad 41	Sicilian White Beans And Escarole 31
6	Lime'd Blueberries 21	Italian Veggie Beef Soup 50	Tasty Lentil Tacos 37
7	Chickpeas With Garlic And Parsley 31	Sausage-topped White Pizza 55	Hearty Vegetable Lentil Soup 51
8	Light Parmesan Pasta 36	Raspberry Peach Puff Pancake 16	Cheesy Shrimp And Grits 27
9	Warm Spinach Salad With Feta And Pistachios 41	Cool & Crunchy Chicken Salad 56	Spicy Barbecued Chicken 55
10	Lemony Asparagus Spear Salad 42	Maple Apple Baked Oatmeal 18	Skillet-grilled Meatless Burgers With Spicy Sour Cream 38
11	Crostini With Kalamata Tomato 22	Creamy Butternut Soup 50	Balsamic Chicken With Roasted Tomatoes 56
12	Saucy Spiced Pears 64	Squash Melt 69	Strawberry Pot Stickers 66
13	Cumin'd Salsa Salad 41	Nectarines And Berries In Prosecco 66	Gazpacho Salad 42
14	Tomato-jalapeno Granita 22	Guacamole 18	Crunchy Tuna Wraps 26

DAY	Breakfast	Lunch	Dinner
15	Asian Marinated Mushrooms 23	Avocado & Garbanzo Bean Quinoa Salad 36	Brown Rice With Tomatoes And Chickpeas 33
16	Frozen Yogurt Fruit Pops 65	Cold-day Chicken Noodle Soup 52	Black Beans With Bell Peppers & Rice 38
17	No-fuss Banana Ice Cream 65	Fresh Lemon Roasted Brussels Sprouts 69	Citrus-spiced Roast Chicken 56
18	Roasted Beans And Green Onions 70	Chunky Veggie Slaw 42	Sausage & Greens Soup 51
19	Parmesan Butternut Squash 70	Teriyaki Beef Stew 60	Fig Bars 64
20	Confetti Corn 70	Citrus-spiced Roast Chicken 56	Seared Scallops With Snap Pea And Edamame Slaw 28
21	Chinese Starter Soup 50	Sassy Salsa Meat Loaves 47	Smoky Cauliflower 69
22	Sautéed Zucchini Ribbons 71	Carne Guisada 61	Chicken Tortilla Soup With Greens 52
23	Tomato Topper Over Anything 36	Spiced Pork Tenderloin With Carrots Slow Cooker Beef Tostadas 60	Braised Swiss Chard With Shiitakes And Peanuts 59
24	Balsamic-goat Cheese Grilled Plums 23	Chickpeas With Garlic And Parsley 31	Chicken Thighs With Black-eyed Pea Ragout 59
25	Hot Skillet Pineapple 71	Parmesan Potato Bake 33	Wheat Berry Salad With Roasted Red Pepper, Feta, And Arugula 32
26	Fresh Fruit Combo 16	Sicilian White Beans And Escarole 31	And Radishes 60
27	Smoky Sirloin 46	Greek-style Ravioli 45	Garlic Pork Roast 46
28	Open-faced Roast Beef Sandwiches 45	Weeknight Pasta 45	One-pot Beef & Pepper Stew 47

Breakfast Recipes

Recipe

....

From the kicthen of ....

Serves .... Prep time .... Cook time ....

☐ Difficulty   ☐ Easy   ☐ Medium   ☐ Hard

Ingredient

Yummy!

....

....

....

....

....

....

Directions ....

....

....

....

....

....

....

Breakfast Recipes

Fresh Fruit Combo

Servings:14 | Cooking Time: 20 Minutes

Ingredients:

- 2 cups cubed fresh pineapple
- 2 medium oranges, peeled and chopped
- 3 kiwifruit, peeled and sliced
- 1 cup sliced fresh strawberries
- 1 cup halved seedless red grapes
- 2 medium firm bananas, sliced
- 1 large red apple, cubed
- 1 cup fresh or frozen blueberries
- 1 cup fresh or canned pitted dark sweet cherries

Directions:

1. In a large bowl, combine the first five ingredients; refrigerate until serving. When ready to serve, fold in bananas, apple, blueberries and cherries.

Nutrition Info:

- Info78 cal., 0 fat (0 sat. fat), 0 chol., 3mg sod., 20g carb. (13g sugars, 3g fiber), 1g pro.

Apple Spiced Tea

Servings:1 | Cooking Time: 10 Minutes

Ingredients:

- 1/2 cup apple cider or juice
- 1/4 teaspoon minced fresh gingerroot
- 2 whole allspice
- 2 whole cloves
- 1 black tea bag
- 1/2 cup boiling water
- 1 tablespoon brown sugar

Directions:

1. In a small bowl, combine the first five ingredients. Add boiling water. Cover and steep for 5 minutes. Strain, discarding tea bag and spices. Stir in sugar. Serve immediately.

Nutrition Info:

- Info112 cal., 0 fat (0 sat. fat), 0 chol., 12mg sod., 28g carb. (27g sugars, 0 fiber), 0 pro.

Raspberry Peach Puff Pancake

Servings:4 | Cooking Time: 20 Minutes

Ingredients:

- 2 medium peaches, peeled and sliced
- 1/2 teaspoon sugar
- 1/2 cup fresh raspberries
- 1 tablespoon butter
- 3 large eggs, lightly beaten
- 1/2 cup fat-free milk
- 1/8 teaspoon salt
- 1/2 cup all-purpose flour
- 1/4 cup vanilla yogurt

Directions:

1. Preheat oven to 400°. In a small bowl, toss peaches with sugar; gently stir in raspberries.
2. Place butter in a 9-in. pie plate; heat in oven 2-3 minutes or until butter is melted. Meanwhile, in a small bowl, whisk eggs, milk and salt until blended; gradually whisk in in flour. Remove pie plate from the oven; tilt carefully, coating bottom and sides with butter. Immediately pour in egg mixture.
3. Bake 18-22 minutes or until puffed and browned. Remove pancake from the oven. Serve immediately with fruit mixture and yogurt.

Nutrition Info:

- Info199 cal., 7g fat (3g sat. fat), 149mg chol., 173mg sod., 25g carb. (11g sugars, 3g fiber), 9g pro.

Calico Scrambled Eggs

Servings:4 | Cooking Time: 15 Minutes

Ingredients:

- 8 large eggs
- 1/4 cup 2% milk
- 1/8 to 1/4 teaspoon dill weed
- 1/8 to 1/4 teaspoon salt
- 1/8 to 1/4 teaspoon pepper
- 1 tablespoon butter
- 1/2 cup chopped green pepper
- 1/4 cup chopped onion
- 1/2 cup chopped fresh tomato

Directions:

1. In a bowl, whisk the first five ingredients until blended. In a 12-in. nonstick skillet, heat butter over medium-high heat. Add green pepper and onion; cook and stir until tender. Remove from pan.

2. In same pan, pour in egg mixture; cook and stir over medium heat until eggs begin to thicken. Add tomato and pepper mixture; cook until heated through and no liquid egg remains, stirring gently.

Nutrition Info:

- Info188 cal., 13g fat (5g sat. fat), 381mg chol., 248mg sod., 4g carb. (3g sugars, 1g fiber), 14g pro.

Mixed Fruit With Lemon-basil Dressing

Servings:8 | Cooking Time: 15 Minutes

Ingredients:

- 2 tablespoons lemon juice
- 1/2 teaspoon sugar
- 1/4 teaspoon salt
- 1/4 teaspoon ground mustard
- 1/8 teaspoon onion powder
- Dash pepper
- 6 tablespoons olive oil
- 4 1/2 teaspoons minced fresh basil
- 1 cup cubed fresh pineapple
- 1 cup sliced fresh strawberries
- 1 cup sliced peeled kiwifruit
- 1 cup cubed seedless watermelon
- 1 cup fresh blueberries
- 1 cup fresh raspberries

Directions:

1. In a blender, combine the lemon juice, sugar, salt, mustard, onion powder and pepper; cover and process for 5 seconds. While processing, gradually add oil in a steady stream. Stir in basil.

2. In a large bowl, combine the fruit. Drizzle with dressing and toss to coat. Refrigerate until serving.

Nutrition Info:

- Info145 cal., 11g fat (1g sat. fat), 0 chol., 76mg sod., 14g carb. (9g sugars, 3g fiber), 1g pro.

Maple Apple Baked Oatmeal

Servings:8 | Cooking Time: 25 Minutes

Ingredients:

- 3 cups old-fashioned oats
- 2 teaspoons baking powder
- 1 1/4 teaspoons ground cinnamon
- 1/2 teaspoon salt
- 1/4 teaspoon ground nutmeg
- 2 large eggs
- 2 cups fat-free milk
- 1/2 cup maple syrup
- 1/4 cup canola oil
- 1 teaspoon vanilla extract
- 1 large apple, chopped
- 1/4 cup sunflower kernels or pepitas

Directions:

1. Preheat oven to 350°. In a large bowl, mix the first five ingredients. In a small bowl, whisk eggs, milk, syrup, oil and vanilla until blended; stir into dry ingredients. Let stand 5 minutes. Stir in apple.
2. Transfer to an 11x7-in. baking dish coated with cooking spray. Sprinkle with sunflower kernels. Bake, uncovered, 25-30 minutes or until set and edges are lightly browned.

Nutrition Info:

- Info305 cal., 13g fat (2g sat. fat), 48mg chol., 325mg sod., 41g carb. (20g sugars, 4g fiber), 8g pro.

Guacamole

Servings:2 | Cooking Time:28minutes

Ingredients:

- 2 tablespoons finely chopped onion
- 1 serrano chile, stemmed, seeded, and minced
- 1 teaspoon kosher salt
- ¼ teaspoon grated lime zest plus 1½–2 tablespoons juice
- 3 ripe avocados, halved, pitted, and cut into ½-inch pieces
- 1 plum tomato, cored, seeded, and minced
- 2 tablespoons chopped fresh cilantro

Directions:

1. Place onion, serrano, salt, and lime zest on cutting board and chop until very finely minced. Transfer onion mixture to medium serving bowl and stir in 1½ tablespoons lime juice. Add avocados and, using sturdy whisk, mash and stir mixture until well combined with some ¼- to ½-inch chunks of avocado remaining. Stir in tomato and cilantro. (Guacamole can be refrigerated for up to 1 day by pressing plastic wrap directly against its surface.) Season with up to additional 1½ teaspoons lime juice to taste before serving.

Nutrition Info:

- Info120 cal., 11g fat (1g sag. fat), 0mg chol, 160mg sod., 7g carb (1g sugars, 5g fiber), 2g pro.

Appetizers And Snacks

RECIPES

DATE

RECIPES		Salads	Meats	Soups
SERVES		Grains	Seafood	Snack
PREP TIME		Breads	Vegetables	Breakfast
COOK TIME		Appetizers	Desserts	Lunch
FROM THE KITCHEN OF		Main Dishes	Beverages	Dinners

INGREDIENTS

_____

_____

_____

_____

DIRECTIONS

_____

_____

_____

_____

_____

_____

_____

NOTES

SERVING	☆☆☆☆☆
DIFFICULTY	☆☆☆☆☆
OVERALL	☆☆☆☆☆

Appetizers And Snacks

Cheesy Snack Mix

Servings:2 | Cooking Time: 5 Minutes

Ingredients:

- 3 cups Corn Chex
- 3 cups Rice Chex
- 3 cups cheddar miniature pretzels
- 1/4 cup butter, melted
- 1 envelope cheesy taco seasoning
- 2 cups white cheddar popcorn

Directions:

1. In a large microwave-safe bowl, combine cereal and pretzels. In a small bowl, mix melted butter and taco seasoning; drizzle over cereal mixture and toss to coat.
2. Microwave, uncovered, on high 3-3 1/2 minutes or until heated through, stirring once every minute. Stir in popcorn. Transfer to a baking sheet to cool completely. Store snack mix in an airtight container.

Nutrition Info:

- Info151 cal., 5g fat (3g sat. fat), 11mg chol., 362mg sod., 23g carb. (2g sugars, 1g fiber), 3g pro.

Pickled Shrimp With Basil

Servings:20 | Cooking Time: 15 Minutes

Ingredients:

- 1/2 cup red wine vinegar
- 1/2 cup olive oil
- 2 teaspoons seafood seasoning
- 2 teaspoons stone-ground mustard
- 1 garlic clove, minced
- 2 pounds peeled and deveined cooked shrimp (31-40 per pound)
- 1 medium lemon, thinly sliced
- 1 medium lime, thinly sliced
- 1/2 medium red onion, thinly sliced
- 1/4 cup thinly sliced fresh basil

- 2 tablespoons capers, drained
- 1/4 cup minced fresh basil
- 1/2 teaspoon kosher salt
- 1/4 teaspoon coarsely ground pepper

Directions:

1. In a large bowl, whisk the first five ingredients. Add shrimp, lemon, lime, onion, sliced basil and capers; toss gently to coat. Refrigerate, covered, up to 8 hours, stirring occasionally.
2. Just before serving, stir minced basil, salt and pepper into the shrimp mixture. Serve with a slotted spoon.

Nutrition Info:

- Info64 cal., 2g fat (0 sat. fat), 69mg chol., 111mg sod., 1g carb. (0 sugars, 0 fiber), 9g pro.

Lime'd Blueberries

Servings: 6 | Cooking Time: 5 Minutes

Ingredients:

- 2 cups frozen unsweetened blueberries, partially thawed
- 1/4 cup frozen grape juice concentrate
- 1 1/2 tablespoons lime juice

Directions:

1. Place all ingredients in a medium bowl and toss gently.
2. Serve immediately for peak flavor and texture.

Nutrition Info:

- Info50 cal., 0g fat (0g sag. fat), 0mg chol, 5mg sod., 13g carb (11g sugars, 1g fiber), 0g pro.

Garden-fresh Wraps

Servings:8 | Cooking Time: 20 Minutes

Ingredients:

- 1 medium ear sweet corn
- 1 medium cucumber, chopped
- 1 cup shredded cabbage
- 1 medium tomato, chopped
- 1 small red onion, chopped
- 1 jalapeno pepper, seeded and minced
- 1 tablespoon minced fresh basil
- 1 tablespoon minced fresh cilantro
- 1 tablespoon minced fresh mint
- 1/3 cup Thai chili sauce
- 3 tablespoons rice vinegar
- 2 teaspoons reduced-sodium soy sauce
- 2 teaspoons creamy peanut butter
- 8 Bibb or Boston lettuce leaves

Directions:

1. Cut corn from cob and place in a large bowl. Add cucumber, cabbage, tomato, onion, jalapeno and herbs.
2. Whisk together chili sauce, vinegar, soy sauce and peanut butter. Pour over vegetable mixture; toss to coat. Let stand 20 minutes.
3. Using a slotted spoon, place 1/2 cup salad in each lettuce leaf. Fold lettuce over filling.

Nutrition Info:

- Info64 cal., 1g fat (0 sat. fat), 0 chol., 319mg sod., 13g carb. (10g sugars, 2g fiber), 2g pro.

Tomato-jalapeno Granita

Servings:6 | Cooking Time: 15 Minutes

Ingredients:

- 2 cups tomato juice
- 1/3 cup sugar
- 4 mint sprigs
- 1 jalapeno pepper, sliced
- 2 tablespoons lime juice
- Fresh mint leaves, optional

Directions:

1. In a small saucepan, bring the tomato juice, sugar, mint sprigs and jalapeno to a boil. Cook and stir until sugar is dissolved. Remove from the heat; cover and let stand 15 minutes.
2. Strain and discard solids. Stir in lime juice. Transfer to a 1-qt. dish; cool to room temperature. Freeze for 1 hour; stir with a fork.
3. Freeze 2-3 hours longer or until completely frozen, stirring every 30 minutes. Scrape granita with a fork just before serving; spoon into dessert dishes. If desired garnish with additional mint leaves.

Nutrition Info:

- Info59 cal., 0 fat (0 sat. fat), 0 chol., 205mg sod., 15g carb. (13g sugars, 0 fiber), 1g pro.

Crostini With Kalamata Tomato

Servings: 4 | Cooking Time:10 Minutes

Ingredients:

- 4 ounces multigrain baguette bread, cut in 12 slices (about 1/4 inch thick)
- 1 small tomato, finely chopped
- 9 small kalamata olives, pitted and finely chopped
- 2 tablespoons chopped fresh basil

Directions:

1. Preheat the oven to 350°F.
2. Arrange the bread slices on a baking sheet and bake 10 minutes or until just golden on the edges. Remove from the heat and cool completely.
3. Meanwhile, stir the remaining ingredients together in a small bowl. Spread 1 tablespoon of the mixture on each bread slice.

Nutrition Info:

- Info90 cal., 2g fat (0g sag. fat), 0mg chol, 220mg sod., 16g carb (2g sugars, 1g fiber), 3g pro.

Mango Avocado Spring Rolls

Servings:8 | Cooking Time: 40 Minutes

Ingredients:

- 4 ounces reduced-fat cream cheese
- 2 tablespoons lime juice
- 1 teaspoon Sriracha Asian hot chili sauce or 1/2 teaspoon hot pepper sauce
- 1 medium sweet red pepper, finely chopped
- 2/3 cup cubed avocado
- 3 green onions, thinly sliced
- 1/3 cup chopped fresh cilantro
- 8 round rice paper wrappers (8 inches)
- 1 medium mango, peeled and thinly sliced
- 2 cups alfalfa sprouts

Directions:

1. Mix cream cheese, lime juice and chili sauce; gently stir in pepper, avocado, green onions and cilantro.
2. Fill a large shallow dish partway with water. Dip a rice paper wrapper into water just until pliable, about 45 seconds (do not soften completely); allow excess water to drip off.
3. Place wrapper on a flat surface. Place cream cheese mixture, mango and sprouts across bottom third of wrapper. Fold in both ends of wrapper; fold bottom side over filling, then roll up tightly. Place on a serving plate, seam side down. Repeat with remaining ingredients. Serve immediately.

Nutrition Info:

- Info117 cal., 5g fat (2g sat. fat), 10mg chol., 86mg sod., 16g carb. (6g sugars, 2g fiber), 3g pro.

Balsamic-goat Cheese Grilled Plums

Servings:8 | Cooking Time: 25 Minutes

Ingredients:

- 1 cup balsamic vinegar
- 2 teaspoons grated lemon peel
- 4 medium firm plums, halved and pitted
- 1/2 cup crumbled goat cheese

Directions:

1. For glaze, in a small saucepan, combine vinegar and lemon peel; bring to a boil. Cook 10-12 minutes or until mixture is thickened and reduced to about 1/3 cup (do not overcook).
2. Grill plums, covered, over medium heat 2-3 minutes on each side or until tender. Drizzle with glaze; top with goat cheese.

Nutrition Info:

- Info58 cal., 2g fat (1g sat. fat), 9mg chol., 41mg sod., 9g carb. (8g sugars, 1g fiber), 2g pro.

Asian Marinated Mushrooms

Servings: 4 | Cooking Time:8 Minutes

Ingredients:

- 8 ounces whole medium mushrooms, stemmed and wiped clean with damp paper towel
- 1/4 tablespoons lite soy sauce
- 2 tablespoons lime juice
- 1 teaspoon extra virgin olive oil

Directions:

1. Place the mushrooms, soy sauce, lime juice, and oil in a large plastic zippered bag. Seal the bag and shake to coat completely. Let stand 30 minutes. Meanwhile, preheat the broiler.
2. Place mushroom mixture (with marinade) in an 8-inch pie pan or baking pan and broil 4 inches away from heat source for 8 minutes or until the mushrooms begin to brown, stirring frequently.
3. Serve with wooden toothpicks and marinade. Top with 2 tablespoons chopped fresh parsley, if desired.

Nutrition Info:

- Info30 cal., 1g fat (0g sag. fat), 0mg chol, 240mg sod., 3g carb (1g sugars, 1g fiber), 2g pro.

Fish & Seafood Recipes

Recipe ....

From the kicthen of ....

Serves .... Prep time .... Cook time ....

☐ Difficulty   ☐ Easy   ☐ Medium   ☐ Hard

Ingredient

....

....

....

....

....

Directions ....

....

....

....

....

....

Fish & Seafood Recipes

Tomato-poached Halibut

Servings:4 | Cooking Time: 30 Minutes

Ingredients:

- 1 tablespoon olive oil
- 2 poblano peppers, finely chopped
- 1 small onion, finely chopped
- 1 can (14 1/2 ounces) fire-roasted diced tomatoes, undrained
- 1 can (14 1/2 ounces) no-salt-added diced tomatoes, undrained
- 1/4 cup chopped pitted green olives
- 3 garlic cloves, minced
- 1/4 teaspoon pepper
- 1/8 teaspoon salt
- 4 halibut fillets (4 ounces each)
- 1/3 cup chopped fresh cilantro
- 4 lemon wedges
- Crusty whole grain bread, optional

Directions:

1. In a large nonstick skillet, heat oil over medium-high heat. Add poblano peppers and onion; cook and stir about 4-6 minutes or until tender.
2. Stir in tomatoes, olives, garlic, pepper and salt. Bring to a boil. Adjust heat to maintain a gentle simmer. Add fillets. Cook, covered, 8-10 minutes or until fish just begins to flake easily with a fork. Sprinkle with cilantro. Serve with lemon wedges and, if desired, bread.

Nutrition Info:

- Info224 cal., 7g fat (1g sat. fat), 56mg chol., 651mg sod., 17g carb. (8g sugars, 4g fiber), 24g pro.

Crunchy Tuna Wraps

Servings:2 | Cooking Time: 10 Minutes

Ingredients:

- 1 pouch (6.4 ounces) light tuna in water
- 1/4 cup finely chopped celery
- 1/4 cup chopped green onions
- 1/4 cup sliced water chestnuts, chopped
- 3 tablespoons chopped sweet red pepper
- 2 tablespoons reduced-fat mayonnaise
- 2 teaspoons prepared mustard
- 2 spinach tortillas (8 inches), room temperature
- 1 cup shredded lettuce

Directions:

1. In a small bowl, mix the first seven ingredients until blended. Spread over tortillas; sprinkle with lettuce. Roll up tightly jelly-roll style.

Nutrition Info:

- Info312 cal., 10g fat (2g sat. fat), 38mg chol., 628mg sod., 34g carb. (2g sugars, 3g fiber), 23g pro.

Fantastic Fish Tacos

Servings:4 | Cooking Time: 30 Minutes

Ingredients:

- 1/2 cup fat-free mayonnaise
- 1 tablespoon lime juice
- 2 teaspoons fat-free milk
- 1 large egg
- 1 teaspoon water
- 1/3 cup dry bread crumbs
- 2 tablespoons salt-free lemon-pepper seasoning
- 1 pound mahi mahi or cod fillets, cut into 1-inch strips
- 4 corn tortillas (6 inches), warmed
- TOPPINGS
- 1 cup coleslaw mix
- 2 medium tomatoes, chopped
- 1 cup shredded reduced-fat Mexican cheese blend
- 1 tablespoon minced fresh cilantro

Directions:

1. For the sauce, in a small bowl, mix the mayonnaise, lime juice and milk; refrigerate until serving.
2. In a shallow bowl, whisk together egg and water. In another bowl, toss bread crumbs with lemon pepper. Dip fish in egg mixture, then in crumb mixture, patting to help coating adhere.
3. Place a large nonstick skillet coated with cooking spray over medium-high heat. Add fish; cook 2-4 minutes per side or until golden brown and fish just begins to flake easily with a fork. Serve in tortillas with toppings and sauce.

Nutrition Info:

- Info321 cal., 10g fat (5g sat. fat), 148mg chol., 632mg sod., 29g carb. (5g sugars, 4g fiber), 34g pro.

Cheesy Shrimp And Grits

Servings:4 | Cooking Time:30 Minutes

Ingredients:

- 1 tablespoon extra-virgin olive oil
- 3 scallions, white parts sliced thin, green parts sliced thin on bias
- 2 garlic cloves, minced
- 1 teaspoon minced canned chipotle chile in adobo sauce
- 4 cups water
- ½ cup 1 percent low-fat milk
- Salt and pepper
- 1 cup old-fashioned grits
- 2 ounces sharp cheddar cheese, shredded (½ cup)
- 1½ pounds extra-large shrimp (21 to 25 per pound), peeled and deveined
- Lemon wedges

Directions:

1. Adjust oven rack to middle position and heat oven to 450 degrees. Heat oil in medium saucepan over medium heat until shimmering. Add scallion whites and cook until softened, about 2 minutes. Stir in garlic and chipotle and cook until fragrant, about 30 seconds. Stir in water, milk, and pinch salt and bring to boil. Slowly whisk in grits. Reduce heat to low and cook, stirring often, until grits are thick and creamy, about 15 minutes.
2. Off heat, stir in cheese, ⅛ teaspoon salt, and ⅛ teaspoon pepper, then transfer to 13 by 9-inch baking dish. Nestle shrimp into grits, leaving tails exposed. Bake until shrimp are cooked through, about 15 minutes. Let cool slightly, then sprinkle with scallion greens. Serve with lemon wedges.

Nutrition Info:

- Info330 cal., 10g fat (4g sag. fat), 175mg chol, 380mg sod., 32g carb (2g sugars, 3g fiber), 25g pro.

Creamy Chipotle Chile Sauce

Servings:1 | Cooking Time:1week

Ingredients:

- You can vary the spiciness of this sauce by adjusting the amount of chipotle.
- ¼ cup mayonnaise
- 2 tablespoons low-fat sour cream
- 1 tablespoon lime juice
- 2 teaspoons minced fresh cilantro
- 1 garlic clove, minced
- ½ teaspoon minced canned chipotle chile in adobo sauce
- Water
- Pepper

Directions:

1. Combine mayonnaise, sour cream, lime juice, cilantro, garlic, and chipotle in bowl. Add water as needed to thin sauce consistency and season with pepper to taste. Cover and refrigerate for 30 minutes before serving. (Sauce can be refrigerated for up to 24 hours.)

Nutrition Info:

- Info100 cal., 11g fat (2g sag. fat), 5mg chol, 95mg sod., 1g carb (1g sugars, 0g fiber), 1g pro.

Seared Scallops With Snap Pea And Edamame Slaw

Servings:4 | Cooking Time: 10 Minutes

Ingredients:

- 3 tablespoons chopped fresh chives
- 2 tablespoons plain low-fat yogurt
- 2 tablespoons mayonnaise
- ½ teaspoon grated lemon zest plus 1 tablespoon juice
- Salt and pepper
- 12 ounces sugar snap peas, strings removed and sliced thin on bias
- 10 ounces frozen edamame, thawed
- 1 English cucumber, halved lengthwise, seeded, and sliced thin
- 6 radishes, trimmed, halved lengthwise, and sliced thin
- 1½ pounds large sea scallops, tendons removed
- 2 tablespoons canola oil

Directions:

1. Whisk chives, yogurt, mayonnaise, lemon zest and juice, and ⅛ teaspoon salt together in large bowl. Add snap peas, edamame, cucumber, and radishes and stir to coat; set aside.

2. Place scallops in rimmed baking sheet lined with clean kitchen towel. Place second clean kitchen towel on top of scallops and press gently on towel to blot liquid. Let scallops sit at room temperature, covered with towel, for 10 minutes. Sprinkle scallops with ⅛ teaspoon salt and ⅛ teaspoon pepper.

3. Heat 1 tablespoon oil in 12-inch nonstick skillet over medium heat until just smoking. Add half of scallops and cook, without moving them, until well browned on first side, about 1½ minutes. Flip scallops and continue to cook, without moving them, until well browned on second side, sides are firm, and centers are opaque, about 1½ minutes. Transfer scallops to serving platter and tent loosely with aluminum foil. Repeat with remaining 1 tablespoon oil and remaining scallops. Serve scallops with slaw.

Nutrition Info:

- Info360 cal., 16g fat (1g sag. fat), 45mg chol, 480mg sod., 22g carb (8g sugars, 6g fiber), 32g pro.

Potatoes, Pasta, And Whole Grains

Recipe

....

From the kicthen of ....

Serves .... Prep time .... Cook time ....

☐ Difficulty ☐ Easy ☐ Medium ☐ Hard

Yummy!

Ingredient

....

....

....

....

....

....

Directions ....

....

....

....

....

....

....

Potatoes, Pasta, And Whole Grains

Chickpeas With Garlic And Parsley

Servings:4 | Cooking Time:7 Minutes

Ingredients:

- 3 tablespoons extra-virgin olive oil
- 4 garlic cloves, sliced thin
- ⅛ teaspoon red pepper flakes
- 1 onion, chopped fine
- Salt and pepper
- 2 (15-ounce) cans no-salt-added chickpeas, rinsed
- 1 cup unsalted chicken broth
- 2 tablespoons minced fresh parsley
- 2 teaspoons lemon juice

Directions:

1. Cook 2 tablespoons oil, garlic, and pepper flakes in 12-inch skillet over medium heat, stirring frequently, until garlic turns golden but not brown, about 3 minutes. Stir in onion and ¼ teaspoon salt and cook until softened and lightly browned, 5 to 7 minutes. Stir in chickpeas and broth and bring to simmer. Reduce heat to medium-low, cover, and cook until chickpeas are heated through and flavors meld, about 7 minutes.
2. Uncover, increase heat to high, and continue to cook until nearly all liquid has evaporated, about 3 minutes. Off heat, stir in parsley and lemon juice. Season with pepper to taste and drizzle with remaining 1 tablespoon oil. Serve.

Nutrition Info:

- Info260 cal., 12g fat (1g sag. fat), 0mg chol, 210mg sod., 27g carb (3g sugars, 6g fiber), 9g pro.

Sicilian White Beans And Escarole

Servings:6 | Cooking Time:25 Minutes

Ingredients:

- 2 tablespoons extra-virgin olive oil
- 2 onions, chopped fine
- Salt and pepper
- 4 garlic cloves, minced
- ⅛ teaspoon red pepper flakes
- 1 head escarole (1 pound), trimmed and sliced 1 inch thick
- 1 (15-ounce) can no-salt-added cannellini beans, rinsed
- 1 cup unsalted chicken broth
- 1 cup water
- 2 teaspoons lemon juice

Directions:

1. Heat 1 tablespoon oil in Dutch oven over medium heat until shimmering. Add onions and ¼ teaspoon salt and cook until softened and lightly browned, 5 to 7 minutes. Stir in garlic and pepper flakes and cook until fragrant, about 30 seconds.
2. Stir in escarole, beans, broth, and water and bring to simmer. Cook, stirring occasionally, until escarole is wilted, about 5 minutes. Increase heat to high and cook until liquid is nearly evaporated, 10 to 15 minutes. Stir in lemon juice and season with pepper to taste. Drizzle with remaining 1 tablespoon oil and serve.

Nutrition Info:

- Info110 cal., 5g fat (0g sag. fat), 0mg chol, 150mg sod., 13g carb (2g sugars, 5g fiber), 4g pro.

Warm Farro With Mushrooms And Thyme

Servings:6 | Cooking Time: 30 Minutes

Ingredients:

- 1½ cups whole farro
- Salt and pepper
- 3 tablespoons extra-virgin olive oil
- 12 ounces cremini mushrooms, trimmed and chopped coarse
- 1 shallot, minced
- 1½ teaspoons minced fresh thyme or ½ teaspoon dried
- 3 tablespoons dry sherry
- 3 tablespoons minced fresh parsley
- 1½ teaspoons sherry vinegar, plus extra for seasoning

Directions:

1. Bring 4 quarts water to boil in large pot. Add farro and 1 teaspoon salt and cook until grains are tender with slight chew, 15 to 30 minutes. Drain farro, return to now-empty pot, and cover to keep warm.
2. Heat 2 tablespoons oil in 12-inch skillet over medium heat until shimmering. Add mushrooms, shallot, thyme, and ¼ teaspoon salt and cook, stirring occasionally, until moisture has evaporated and vegetables start to brown, 8 to 10 minutes. Stir in sherry, scraping up any browned bits, and cook until skillet is almost dry.
3. Add farro and remaining 1 tablespoon oil and cook until heated through, about 2 minutes. Off heat, stir in parsley and vinegar. Season with pepper and extra vinegar to taste and serve.

Nutrition Info:

- Info250 cal., 9g fat (1g sag. fat), 0mg chol, 135mg sod., 39g carb (4g sugars, 4g fiber), 7g pro.

Wheat Berry Salad With Roasted Red Pepper, Feta, And Arugula

Servings:6 | Cooking Time: 70 Minutes

Ingredients:

- 1 cup wheat berries
- Salt
- 2 tablespoons extra-virgin olive oil
- 2 tablespoons sherry vinegar
- 2 garlic cloves, minced
- ½ teaspoon ground cumin
- ⅛ teaspoon cayenne pepper
- 1 (15-ounce) can no-salt-added chickpeas, rinsed
- ½ cup jarred roasted red peppers, rinsed, patted dry, and chopped
- 2 ounces feta cheese, crumbled (½ cup)
- ¼ cup minced fresh cilantro
- 2 ounces (2 cups) baby arugula, chopped coarse

Directions:

1. Bring 4 quarts water to boil in large pot. Add wheat berries and ½ teaspoon salt and cook until tender with slight chew, 60 to 70 minutes.
2. Whisk oil, vinegar, garlic, cumin, and cayenne together in large bowl. Drain wheat berries, add to bowl with dressing, and gently toss to coat. Let cool slightly, about 15 minutes.
3. Stir in chickpeas, red peppers, feta, and cilantro. Add arugula and gently toss to combine. Serve.

Nutrition Info:

- Info230 cal., 7g fat (2g sag. fat), 10mg chol, 170mg sod., 32g carb (2g sugars, 6g fiber), 8g pro.

Brown Rice With Tomatoes And Chickpeas

Servings:8 | Cooking Time:30 Minutes

Ingredients:

- 12 ounces grape tomatoes, quartered
- 5 scallions, sliced thin
- ¼ cup minced fresh cilantro
- 4 teaspoons extra-virgin olive oil
- 1 tablespoon lime juice
- Salt and pepper
- 2 red bell peppers, stemmed, seeded, and chopped fine
- 1 onion, chopped fine
- 1 cup long-grain brown rice, rinsed
- 4 garlic cloves, minced
- Pinch saffron threads, crumbled
- Pinch cayenne pepper
- 3¼ cups unsalted chicken broth
- 1 (15-ounce) can no-salt-added chickpeas, rinsed

Directions:

1. Combine tomatoes, scallions, cilantro, 2 teaspoons oil, lime juice, ⅛ teaspoon salt, and ⅛ teaspoon pepper in bowl; set aside for serving.
2. Heat remaining 2 teaspoons oil in 12-inch skillet over medium heat until shimmering. Add bell peppers, onion, and ¼ teaspoon salt and cook until softened and lightly browned, 8 to 10 minutes. Stir in rice, garlic, saffron, and cayenne and cook until fragrant, about 30 seconds.
3. Stir in broth, scraping up any browned bits, and bring to simmer. Reduce heat to medium-low, cover, and cook, stirring occasionally, for 25 minutes.
4. Stir in chickpeas and ⅛ teaspoon salt, cover, and cook until rice is tender and broth is almost completely absorbed, 25 to 30 minutes. Season with pepper to taste. Serve, topping individual portions with tomato mixture.

Nutrition Info:

- Info180 cal., 3g fat (0g sag. fat), 0mg chol, 210mg sod., 30g carb (4g sugars, 4g fiber), 6g pro.

Parmesan Potato Bake

Servings: 6 | Cooking Time:1 Hour

Ingredients:

- 1 1/2 pounds red potatoes, scrubbed and very thinly sliced
- 1/2 cup finely chopped onion
- 3 tablespoons no-trans-fat margarine (35% vegetable oil; divided use)
- 1/8 teaspoon black pepper (divided use)
- 3 tablespoons grated Parmesan cheese (divided use)
- 1/4 teaspoon salt (divided use)

Directions:

1. Preheat the oven to 375°F.
2. Coat a 9-inch deep-dish pie pan with nonstick cooking spray. Put half the potatoes in the pan, then all of the onions, then half of the remaining ingredients. Place the remaining potatoes on top, add the remaining margarine, and sprinkle with the remaining pepper. Cover with foil and bake 45 minutes.
3. Uncover the potatoes and sprinkle with the remaining Parmesan cheese and salt. Bake uncovered for 15 minutes or until the potatoes are tender when pierced with a fork. Let stand 10 minutes to develop flavors.

Nutrition Info:

- Info120 cal., 3g fat (0g sag. fat), 0mg chol, 190mg sod., 20g carb (2g sugars, 2g fiber), 3g pro.

Vegetarian Recipes

RECIPES

DATE

RECIPES	☐ Salads	☐ Meats	☐ Soups
SERVES	☐ Grains	☐ Seafood	☐ Snack
PREP TIME	☐ Breads	☐ Vegetables	☐ Breakfast
COOK TIME	☐ Appetizers	☐ Desserts	☐ Lunch
FROM THE KITCHEN OF	☐ Main Dishes	☐ Beverages	☐ Dinners

INGREDIENTS

_____
_____
_____
_____

DIRECTIONS

_____
_____
_____
_____
_____
_____
_____

NOTES

SERVING	☆☆☆☆☆
DIFFICULTY	☆☆☆☆☆
OVERALL	☆☆☆☆☆

Vegetarian Recipes

Light Parmesan Pasta

Servings: 4 | Cooking Time:8 Minutes

Ingredients:

- 8 ounces uncooked whole-wheat no-yolk egg noodles
- 1/4–1/3 cup fat-free evaporated milk
- 6 tablespoons grated Parmesan cheese (divided use)
- 1 tablespoon no-trans-fat margarine (35% vegetable oil)
- 1/2 teaspoon salt
- 1/4 teaspoon black pepper

Directions:

1. Cook the pasta according to package directions, omitting any salt or fat.
2. Drain the pasta well and place it in a medium bowl. Add the remaining ingredients except 1 tablespoon Parmesan cheese. Toss to blend, then sprinkle with 1 tablespoon Parmesan on top.

Nutrition Info:

- Info230 cal., 4g fat (1g sag. fat), 5mg chol, 450mg sod., 44g carb (2g sugars, 6g fiber), 12g pro.

Avocado & Garbanzo Bean Quinoa Salad

Servings:6 | Cooking Time: 15 Minutes

Ingredients:

- 1 cup quinoa, rinsed
- 1 can (15 ounces) garbanzo beans or chickpeas, rinsed and drained
- 2 cups cherry tomatoes, halved
- 1 cup (4 ounces) crumbled feta cheese
- 1/2 medium ripe avocado, peeled and cubed
- 4 green onions, chopped (about 1/2 cup)
- DRESSING
- 3 tablespoons white wine vinegar
- 1 teaspoon Dijon mustard
- 1/4 teaspoon kosher salt
- 1/4 teaspoon garlic powder
- 1/4 teaspoon freshly ground pepper
- 1/4 cup olive oil

Directions:

1. Cook quinoa according to package directions; transfer to a large bowl and cool slightly.
2. Add beans, tomatoes, cheese, avocado and green onions to quinoa; gently stir to combine. In a small bowl, whisk the first five dressing ingredients. Gradually whisk in oil until blended. Drizzle over salad; gently toss to coat. Refrigerate leftovers.

Nutrition Info:

- Info328 cal., 17g fat (4g sat. fat), 10mg chol., 378mg sod., 34g carb. (3g sugars, 7g fiber), 11g pro.

Tomato Topper Over Anything

Servings: 3 | Cooking Time:22 Minutes

Ingredients:

- 1 (14.5-ounce) can no-salt-added tomatoes with green pepper and onion
- 1/2 cup chopped roasted red peppers
- 2–3 tablespoons chopped fresh basil
- 2 teaspoons extra virgin olive oil

Directions:

1. Bring the tomatoes and peppers to boil in a medium saucepan. Reduce the heat and simmer, uncovered, for 15 minutes or until slightly thickened, stirring occasionally.
2. Remove the mixture from the heat, stir in the basil and oil, and let stand 5 minutes to develop flavors.

Nutrition Info:

- Info80 cal., 3g fat (0g sag. fat), 0mg chol, 90mg sod., 12g carb (8g sugars, 2g fiber), 2g pro.

Ricotta-stuffed Portobello Mushrooms

Servings:6 | Cooking Time: 30 Minutes

Ingredients:

- 3/4 cup reduced-fat ricotta cheese
- 3/4 cup grated Parmesan cheese, divided
- 1/2 cup shredded part-skim mozzarella cheese
- 2 tablespoons minced fresh parsley
- 1/8 teaspoon pepper
- 6 large portobello mushrooms
- 6 slices large tomato
- 3/4 cup fresh basil leaves
- 3 tablespoons slivered almonds or pine nuts, toasted
- 1 small garlic clove
- 2 tablespoons olive oil
- 2 to 3 teaspoons water

Directions:

1. In a small bowl, mix ricotta cheese, 1/4 cup Parmesan cheese, mozzarella cheese, parsley and pepper. Remove and discard stems from mushrooms; with a spoon, scrape and remove gills. Fill caps with ricotta mixture. Top with tomato slices.
2. Grill, covered, over medium heat 8-10 minutes or until mushrooms are tender. Remove from the grill with a metal spatula.
3. Meanwhile, place basil, almonds and garlic in a small food processor; pulse until chopped. Add remaining Parmesan cheese; pulse just until blended. While processing, gradually add the oil and enough water to reach the desired consistency. Spoon the mixture over stuffed mushrooms before serving.

Nutrition Info:

- Info201 cal., 13g fat (4g sat. fat), 22mg chol., 238mg sod., 9g carb. (5g sugars, 2g fiber), 12g pro.

Tasty Lentil Tacos

Servings:6 | Cooking Time: 40 Minutes

Ingredients:

- 1 teaspoon canola oil
- 1 medium onion, finely chopped
- 1 garlic clove, minced
- 1 cup dried lentils, rinsed
- 1 tablespoon chili powder
- 2 teaspoons ground cumin
- 1 teaspoon dried oregano
- 2 1/2 cups vegetable or reduced-sodium chicken broth
- 1 cup salsa
- 12 taco shells
- 1 1/2 cups shredded lettuce
- 1 cup chopped fresh tomatoes
- 1 1/2 cups shredded reduced-fat cheddar cheese
- 6 tablespoons fat-free sour cream

Directions:

1. In a large nonstick skillet, heat oil over medium heat; saute onion and garlic until tender. Add the lentils and seasonings; cook and stir 1 minute. Stir in broth; bring to a boil. Reduce heat; simmer, covered, until lentils are tender, 25-30 minutes.
2. Cook, uncovered, until mixture is thickened, for 6-8 minutes, stirring occasionally. Mash lentils slightly; stir in salsa and heat through. Serve in taco shells. Top with remaining ingredients.

Nutrition Info:

- Info365 cal., 12g fat (5g sat. fat), 21mg chol., 777mg sod., 44g carb. (5g sugars, 6g fiber), 19g pro.

Black Beans With Bell Peppers & Rice

Servings:6 | Cooking Time: 30 Minutes

Ingredients:

- 1 tablespoon olive oil
- 1 each medium sweet yellow, orange and red pepper, chopped
- 1 large onion, chopped
- 2 garlic cloves, minced
- 2 cans (15 ounces each) black beans, rinsed and drained
- 1 package (8.8 ounces) ready-to-serve brown rice
- 1 1/2 teaspoons ground cumin
- 1/2 teaspoon dried oregano
- 1 1/2 cups (6 ounces) shredded Mexican cheese blend, divided
- 3 tablespoons minced fresh cilantro

Directions:

1. In a large skillet, heat the oil over medium-high heat. Add peppers, onion and garlic; cook and stir 6-8 minutes or until tender. Add beans, rice, cumin and oregano; heat through.
2. Stir in 1 cup cheese; sprinkle with remaining cheese. Remove from heat. Let stand, covered, 5 minutes or until cheese is melted. Sprinkle with cilantro.

Nutrition Info:

- Info347 cal., 12g fat (6g sat. fat), 25mg chol., 477mg sod., 40g carb. (4g sugars, 8g fiber), 15g pro.

Skillet-grilled Meatless Burgers With Spicy Sour Cream

Servings: 4 | Cooking Time:15 Minutes

Ingredients:

- 4 soy protein burgers (preferably the grilled variety)
- 1 1/2 cups thinly sliced onions
- 1/8 teaspoon salt (divided use)
- 1/4 cup fat-free sour cream
- 4–6 drops chipotle-flavored hot sauce

Directions:

1. Place a large nonstick skillet over medium heat until hot. Coat the skillet with nonstick cooking spray, add the patties, and cook 4 minutes on each side. Set the patties aside on a separate plate and cover with foil to keep warm.
2. Coat the skillet with nonstick cooking spray and increase the heat to medium high. Add the onions and 1/16 teaspoon salt. Lightly coat the onions with nonstick cooking spray and cook 5 minutes or until they are richly browned, stirring frequently.
3. Meanwhile, stir the sour cream, hot sauce, and 1/16 teaspoon salt together in a small bowl.
4. When the onions are browned, push them to one side of the skillet and add the patties. Spoon the onions on top of the patties and cook 1–2 minutes longer to heat thoroughly. Top each patty with 1 tablespoon sour cream.

Nutrition Info:

- Info120 cal., 2g fat (0g sag. fat), 5mg chol, 440mg sod., 12g carb (2g sugars, 7g fiber), 16g pro.

Salads Recipes

Recipe

....

From the kicthen of ....

Serves .... Prep time .... Cook time ....

☐ Difficulty   ☐ Easy   ☐ Medium   ☐ Hard

Ingredient

. . . .

. . . .

. . . .

. . . .

. . . .

Directions

. . . .

. . . .

. . . .

. . . .

. . . .

Salads Recipes

Edamame Corn Carrot Salad

Servings:8 | Cooking Time: 25 Minutes

Ingredients:

- 2 1/2 cups frozen shelled edamame
- 3 cups julienned carrots
- 1 1/2 cups frozen corn, thawed
- 4 green onions, chopped
- 2 tablespoons minced fresh cilantro
- VINAIGRETTE
- 3 tablespoons rice vinegar
- 3 tablespoons lemon juice
- 4 teaspoons canola oil
- 2 garlic cloves, minced
- 1/2 teaspoon salt
- 1/2 teaspoon pepper

Directions:

1. Place edamame in a small saucepan; add water to cover. Bring to a boil; cook 4-5 minutes or until tender. Drain and place in a large bowl; cool slightly.
2. Add carrots, corn, green onions and cilantro. Whisk together vinaigrette ingredients; toss with salad. Refrigerate, covered, at least 2 hours before serving.

Nutrition Info:

- Info111 cal., 5g fat (0 sat. fat), 0 chol., 135mg sod., 14g carb. (4g sugars, 3g fiber), 5g pro.

Warm Spinach Salad With Feta And Pistachios

Servings:6 | Cooking Time:15 Minutes

Ingredients:

- 1½ ounces feta cheese, crumbled (⅓ cup)
- 3 tablespoons extra-virgin olive oil
- 1 (3-inch) strip lemon zest plus 1½ tablespoons juice
- 1 shallot, minced
- 10 ounces curly-leaf spinach, stemmed and torn into bite-size pieces

- 6 radishes, trimmed and sliced thin
- 3 tablespoons chopped toasted pistachios
- Pepper

Directions:

1. Place feta on plate and freeze until slightly firm, about 15 minutes.
2. Cook oil, lemon zest, and shallot in Dutch oven over medium-low heat until shallot is softened, about 5 minutes. Off heat, discard zest and stir in lemon juice. Add spinach, cover, and let sit until just beginning to wilt, about 30 seconds.
3. Transfer spinach mixture and liquid left in pot to large bowl. Add radishes, pistachios, and feta and gently toss to coat. Season with pepper to taste. Serve.

Nutrition Info:

- Info120 cal., 10g fat (2g sag. fat), 5mg chol, 105mg sod., 4g carb (1g sugars, 2g fiber), 3g pro.

Cumin'd Salsa Salad

Servings: 4 | Cooking Time: 3 Minutes

Ingredients:

- 3/4 cup mild or medium salsa fresca (pico de gallo)
- 2 tablespoons water
- 1/4 teaspoon ground cumin
- 8 cups shredded lettuce
- 20 baked bite-sized multi-grain tortilla chips, coarsely crumbled (1 ounce)

Directions:

1. Stir the salsa, water, and cumin together in a small bowl.
2. Place 2 cups of lettuce on each of 4 salad plates, spoon 3 tablespoons picante mixture over each salad, and top with chips.

Nutrition Info:

- Info60 cal., 2g fat (0g sag. fat), 0mg chol, 40mg sod., 9g carb (3g sugars, 2g fiber), 2g pro.

Lemony Asparagus Spear Salad

Servings: 4 | Cooking Time:1 Minute

Ingredients:

- 1 pound asparagus spears, trimmed
- 1 tablespoon basil pesto sauce
- 2 teaspoons lemon juice
- 1/4 teaspoon salt

Directions:

1. Cover asparagus with water in a large skillet and bring to a boil, then cover tightly and cook 1 minute or until tender-crisp.
2. Immediately drain the asparagus in a colander and run under cold water to cool. Place the asparagus on paper towels to drain, then place on a serving platter.
3. Top the asparagus with the pesto and roll the spears back and forth to coat completely. Drizzle with lemon juice and sprinkle with salt. Flavors are at their peak if you serve this within 30 minutes.

Nutrition Info:

- Info25 cal., 1g fat (0g sag. fat), 0mg chol, 190mg sod., 3g carb (1g sugars, 1g fiber), 2g pro.

Gazpacho Salad

Servings:6 | Cooking Time:30 Minutes

Ingredients:

- 1 pound cherry tomatoes, quartered
- 1 cucumber, peeled, halved lengthwise, seeded, and cut into ½-inch pieces
- Salt and pepper
- 5 teaspoons extra-virgin olive oil
- 4 teaspoons sherry vinegar
- 1 shallot, minced
- 1 garlic clove, minced
- 1 red bell pepper, stemmed, seeded, and cut into ½-inch pieces
- ¼ cup minced fresh cilantro

Directions:

1. Toss tomatoes and cucumber with ½ teaspoon salt in colander and let drain for 15 to 30 minutes.
2. Whisk oil, vinegar, shallot, and garlic together in large bowl. Add tomato mixture, bell pepper, and cilantro and gently toss to coat. Season with pepper to taste and let sit until flavors meld, about 15 minutes. Serve.

Nutrition Info:

- Info60 cal., 4g fat (0g sag. fat), 0mg chol, 150mg sod., 5g carb (3g sugars, 2g fiber), 1g pro.

Chunky Veggie Slaw

Servings:14 | Cooking Time: 25 Minutes

Ingredients:

- 1 small head cabbage, chopped
- 6 cups fresh broccoli florets
- 1 medium cucumber, chopped
- 2 celery ribs, sliced
- 12 fresh sugar snap peas, halved
- 1 small green pepper, chopped
- 3/4 cup buttermilk
- 1/2 cup reduced-fat mayonnaise
- 3 tablespoons cider vinegar
- 2 tablespoons sugar
- 1/2 teaspoon salt
- 1 cup chopped walnuts, toasted
- 2 green onions, thinly sliced

Directions:

1. In a large bowl, combine the first six ingredients. In a small bowl, whisk buttermilk, mayonnaise, vinegar, sugar and salt. Pour over salad; toss to coat. Top with walnuts and green onions. Refrigerate leftovers.

Nutrition Info:

- Info125 cal., 9g fat (1g sat. fat), 4mg chol., 189mg sod., 10g carb. (6g sugars, 3g fiber), 4g pro.

Meat Recipes

Recipe

....

From the kicthen of ....

Serves .... Prep time .... Cook time ....

☐ Difficulty   ☐ Easy   ☐ Medium   ☐ Hard

Yummy!

Ingredient

....

....

....

....

....

Directions ....

....

....

....

....

....

....

Meat Recipes

Weeknight Pasta

Servings:2 | Cooking Time: 20 Minutes

Ingredients:

- 1/2 pound lean ground beef (90% lean)
- 1 cup sliced fresh mushrooms
- 1/3 cup chopped onion
- 1 garlic clove, minced
- 1 cup gluten-free reduced-sodium beef broth
- 2/3 cup water
- 1/3 cup tomato paste
- 1/2 teaspoon dried basil
- 1/2 teaspoon dried oregano
- 1/8 teaspoon pepper
- 3 ounces uncooked gluten-free spaghetti, broken in half
- 2 teaspoons grated Parmesan cheese

Directions:

1. In a large skillet, cook the beef, mushrooms, onion and garlic over medium heat until meat is no longer pink and vegetables are tender; drain.
2. Stir in broth, water, tomato paste, seasonings and spaghetti. Bring to a boil. Reduce heat; cover and simmer for 15-20 minutes or until spaghetti is tender. Sprinkle with cheese.

Nutrition Info:

- Info412 cal., 11g fat (4g sat. fat), 75mg chol., 335mg sod., 46g carb. (6g sugars, 4g fiber), 31g pro.

Greek-style Ravioli

Servings:2 | Cooking Time: 25 Minutes

Ingredients:

- 12 frozen cheese ravioli
- 1/3 pound lean ground beef (90% lean)
- 1 cup canned diced tomatoes with basil, oregano and garlic

- 1 cup fresh baby spinach
- 1/4 cup sliced ripe olives
- 1/4 cup crumbled feta cheese

Directions:

1. Cook ravioli according to package directions; drain. Meanwhile, in a skillet, cook beef over medium heat for 4-6 minutes or until no longer pink; drain. Stir in tomatoes; bring to a boil. Reduce heat; simmer, uncovered, 10 minutes, stirring occasionally.
2. Add ravioli, spinach and olives; heat through, stirring gently to combine. Sprinkle with cheese.

Nutrition Info:

- Info333 cal., 12g fat (5g sat. fat), 61mg chol., 851mg sod., 28g carb. (5g sugars, 4g fiber), 23g pro.

Open-faced Roast Beef Sandwiches

Servings:8 | Cooking Time: 15 Minutes

Ingredients:

- 1 pound sliced deli roast beef
- 8 slices ciabatta bread (1/2 inch thick)
- 2 cups fresh arugula
- 2 cups torn romaine
- 4 teaspoons olive oil
- 1 tablespoon lemon juice
- 1 tablespoon white wine vinegar
- 1 1/2 teaspoons prepared horseradish

Directions:

1. Place roast beef on ciabatta slices. In a large bowl, combine the arugula and romaine. In a small bowl, whisk the remaining ingredients until blended. Drizzle over greens; toss to coat. Arrange over beef; serve immediately.

Nutrition Info:

- Info150 cal., 5g fat (1g sat. fat), 32mg chol., 422mg sod., 14g carb. (1g sugars, 1g fiber), 14g pro.

Smoky Sirloin

Servings: 4 | Cooking Time:12 Minutes

Ingredients:

- 1 pound boneless sirloin steak, about 3/4-inch thick
- 1 1/2 teaspoons smoked paprika
- 2 tablespoons Worcestershire sauce
- 2 tablespoons balsamic vinegar

Directions:

1. Sprinkle both sides of the beef with paprika, 1/4 teaspoon salt, and 1/4 teaspoon pepper. Press down lightly to adhere. Let stand 15 minutes at room temperature.

2. Heat a large skillet coated with cooking spray over medium-high heat. Cook beef 4 to 5 minutes on each side. Place on cutting board and let stand 5 minutes before slicing.

3. Combine 1/4 cup water, Worcestershire sauce, and vinegar. Pour into the skillet with any pan residue and bring to a boil over medium-high heat. Boil 2 minutes or until reduced to 2 tablespoons liquid. Pour over sliced beef.

Nutrition Info:

- Info150 cal., 3g fat (1g sag. fat), 70mg chol, 280mg sod., 3g carb (2g sugars, 0g fiber), 26g pro.

Garlic Pork Roast

Servings:8 | Cooking Time:20 Minutes

Ingredients:

- 1 (2-pound) boneless center-cut pork loin roast, fat trimmed to ⅛ inch
- 18 garlic cloves (10 peeled and smashed, 8 unpeeled)
- 4 teaspoons extra-virgin olive oil
- Salt and pepper
- 1½ teaspoons minced fresh thyme
- ¼ teaspoon red pepper flakes
- 1 tablespoon unsalted butter

Directions:

1. Slice roast open down middle, from end to end, about two-thirds through pork. Gently press roast open. Carefully slice into sides of roast, being careful not to cut through, and press pork flat. Combine crushed garlic, 1 teaspoon oil, ½ teaspoon salt, and ¼ teaspoon pepper in bowl, then spread mixture evenly over roast. Wrap roast tightly with plastic wrap and refrigerate for at least 1 hour or up to 24 hours.

2. Toast unpeeled garlic cloves in 12-inch skillet over medium heat until fragrant and color deepens slightly, about 8 minutes; set aside. When cool enough to handle, peel garlic. Mince 6 cloves, transfer to bowl, and add 1 teaspoon oil, thyme, pepper flakes, and ¼ teaspoon pepper. Mash mixture to paste with back of fork.

3. Adjust oven rack to lower-middle position and heat oven to 325 degrees. Set wire rack inside aluminum foil–lined rimmed baking sheet. Pat roast dry with paper towels. Spread garlic paste inside surface of pork, leaving ½-inch border on all sides. Wrap sides of pork around garlic paste, then tie at 1½-inch intervals with kitchen twine. Sprinkle with ¼ teaspoon pepper.

4. Heat remaining 2 teaspoons oil in 12-inch skillet over medium-high heat until just smoking. Brown roast on all sides, 6 to 10 minutes. Transfer to prepared rack in baking sheet and roast until pork registers 140 degrees, 50 to 60 minutes.

5. Mince remaining 2 toasted garlic cloves and place in bowl. Add butter and microwave until garlic is golden and butter is melted, about 1 minute, stirring halfway through microwaving. Transfer roast to carving board and brush with garlic butter. Tent with foil and let rest for 15 minutes. Discard twine and slice roast ½ inch thick. Serve.

Nutrition Info:

- Info190 cal., 8g fat (2g sag. fat), 75mg chol, 200mg sod., 2g carb (0g sugars, 0g fiber), 26g pro.

One-pot Beef & Pepper Stew

Servings:8 | Cooking Time: 30 Minutes

Ingredients:

- 1 pound lean ground beef (90% lean)
- 3 cans (14 1/2 ounces each) diced tomatoes, undrained
- 4 large green peppers, coarsely chopped
- 1 large onion, chopped
- 2 cans (4 ounces each) chopped green chilies
- 3 teaspoons garlic powder
- 1 teaspoon pepper
- 1/4 teaspoon salt
- 2 cups uncooked instant rice
- Hot pepper sauce, optional

Directions:

1. In a 6-qt. stockpot, cook beef over medium heat 6-8 minutes or until no longer pink, breaking into crumbles; drain. Add tomatoes, green peppers, onion, chilies and seasonings; bring to a boil. Reduce heat; simmer, covered, for 20-25 minutes or until vegetables are tender.

2. Prepare rice according to package directions. Serve with the stew and, if desired, pepper sauce.

Nutrition Info:

- Info244 cal., 5g fat (2g sat. fat), 35mg chol., 467mg sod., 35g carb. (8g sugars, 5g fiber), 15g pro.

Sassy Salsa Meat Loaves

Servings:2 | Cooking Time: 1 Hour 5 Minutes

Ingredients:

- 3/4 cup uncooked instant brown rice
- 1 can (8 ounces) tomato sauce
- 1 1/2 cups salsa, divided
- 1 large onion, chopped
- 1 large egg, lightly beaten
- 1 celery rib, finely chopped
- 1/4 cup minced fresh parsley
- 2 tablespoons minced fresh cilantro
- 2 garlic cloves, minced
- 1 tablespoon chili powder
- 1 1/2 teaspoons salt
- 1/2 teaspoon pepper
- 2 pounds lean ground beef (90% lean)
- 1 pound ground turkey
- 1/2 cup shredded reduced-fat Monterey Jack cheese or Mexican cheese blend

Directions:

1. Preheat oven to 350°. Cook rice according to package directions; cool slightly. In a large bowl, combine tomato sauce, 1/2 cup salsa, onion, egg, celery, parsley, cilantro, garlic and seasonings; stir in rice. Add beef and turkey; mix lightly but thoroughly.

2. Shape into two 8x4-in. loaves on a greased rack in a broiler pan. Bake 1 to 1 1/4 hours or until a meat thermometer reads 165°.

3. Spread with remaining salsa; sprinkle with cheese; bake 5 minutes or until cheese is melted. Let stand 10 minutes before slicing.

Nutrition Info:

- Info237 cal., 11g fat (4g sat. fat), 91mg chol., 634mg sod., 9g carb. (2g sugars, 1g fiber), 25g pro.

Soups, Stews, And Chilis

RECIPES

DATE

RECIPES		Salads	Meats	Soups
SERVES		Grains	Seafood	Snack
PREP TIME		Breads	Vegetables	Breakfast
COOK TIME		Appetizers	Desserts	Lunch
FROM THE KITCHEN OF		Main Dishes	Beverages	Dinners

INGREDIENTS

DIRECTIONS

NOTES

SERVING	☆☆☆☆☆
DIFFICULTY	☆☆☆☆☆
OVERALL	☆☆☆☆☆

Soups, Stews, And Chilis

Italian Veggie Beef Soup

Servings:12 | Cooking Time: 30 Minutes

Ingredients:

- 1 1/2 pounds lean ground beef (90% lean)
- 2 medium onions, chopped
- 4 cups chopped cabbage
- 1 package (16 ounces) frozen mixed vegetables
- 1 can (28 ounces) crushed tomatoes
- 1 bay leaf
- 3 teaspoons Italian seasoning
- 1 teaspoon salt
- 1/2 teaspoon pepper
- 2 cartons (32 ounces each) reduced-sodium beef broth

Directions:

1. In a 6-qt. stockpot, cook ground beef and onions over medium-high heat for 6-8 minutes or until the beef is no longer pink, breaking up the beef into crumbles; drain.
2. Add cabbage, mixed vegetables, tomatoes, seasonings and broth; bring to a boil. Reduce heat; simmer soup, uncovered, for10-15 minutes or until the cabbage is crisp-tender. Remove bay leaf.

Nutrition Info:

- Info159 cal., 5g fat (2g sat. fat), 38mg chol., 646mg sod., 14g carb. (6g sugars, 4g fiber), 15g pro.

Creamy Butternut Soup

Servings:10 | Cooking Time: 20 Minutes

Ingredients:

- 1 medium butternut squash, peeled, seeded and cubed (about 6 cups)
- 3 medium potatoes (about 1 pound), peeled and cubed
- 1 large onion, diced
- 2 chicken bouillon cubes
- 2 garlic cloves, minced
- 5 cups water
- Sour cream and minced fresh chives, optional

Directions:

1. In a 6-qt. stockpot, combine first six ingredients; bring to a boil. Reduce heat; simmer, covered, until vegetables are tender, 15-20 minutes.
2. Puree soup using an immersion blender. Or, cool slightly and puree soup in batches in a blender; return to pan and heat through. If desired, serve with sour cream and chives.

Nutrition Info:

- Info112 cal., 0 fat (0 sat. fat), 0 chol., 231mg sod., 27g carb. (5g sugars, 4g fiber), 3g pro.

Chinese Starter Soup

Servings: 4 | Cooking Time:10 Minutes

Ingredients:

- 3 cups low-fat, low-sodium chicken broth
- 8 ounces frozen stir-fry vegetables, such as a mix of broccoli, carrots, water chestnuts, and onion
- 2 teaspoons grated gingerroot
- 2 teaspoons lite soy sauce

Directions:

1. In a medium saucepan, bring the broth to boil over high heat. Add the vegetables and return to a boil.
2. Reduce the heat, cover tightly, and simmer 3–4 minutes or until vegetables are tender-crisp.
3. Remove from the heat and add the remaining ingredients. Top with red pepper flakes, if desired. Cover and let stand 3 minutes to develop flavors, then serve.

Nutrition Info:

- Info50 cal., 0g fat (0g sag. fat), 0mg chol, 210mg sod., 7g carb (3g sugars, 1g fiber), 4g pro.

Hearty Vegetable Lentil Soup

Servings:6 | Cooking Time: 45 Minutes

Ingredients:

- 6 bacon strips, chopped
- 1 pound red potatoes (about 3 medium), chopped
- 2 medium carrots, chopped
- 1 medium onion, chopped
- 6 garlic cloves, minced
- 3/4 teaspoon ground cumin
- 1/2 teaspoon salt
- 1/2 teaspoon rubbed sage
- 1/2 teaspoon dried thyme
- 1/4 teaspoon pepper
- 1 1/2 cups dried lentils, rinsed
- 4 cups chicken stock

Directions:

1. In a large saucepan, cook the bacon over medium heat until crisp, stirring occasionally. Remove with a slotted spoon; drain on paper towels. Discard drippings, reserving 1 tablespoon in pan. Add potatoes, carrots and onion; cook and stir 6-8 minutes or until the carrots and onion are tender. Add garlic and seasonings; cook 1 minute longer.
2. Add lentils and stock; bring to a boil. Reduce heat; simmer, covered, 30-35 minutes or until lentils and potatoes are tender. Top each serving with bacon.

Nutrition Info:

- Info314 cal., 6g fat (2g sat. fat), 10mg chol., 708mg sod., 47g carb. (4g sugars, 17g fiber), 20g pro.

Sausage & Greens Soup

Servings:6 | Cooking Time: 20 Minutes

Ingredients:

- 1 tablespoon olive oil
- 2 Italian turkey sausage links (4 ounces each), casings removed
- 1 medium onion, chopped
- 1 celery rib, chopped
- 1 medium carrot, chopped
- 1 garlic clove, minced
- 6 ounces Swiss chard, stems removed, chopped (about 4 cups)
- 1 can (14 1/2 ounces) no-salt-added diced tomatoes, undrained
- 1 bay leaf
- 1 teaspoon rubbed sage
- 1 teaspoon Italian seasoning
- 1/2 teaspoon pepper
- 1 carton (32 ounces) reduced-sodium chicken broth
- 1 can (15 ounces) no-salt-added cannellini beans, rinsed and drained
- 1 tablespoon lemon juice

Directions:

1. In a 6-qt. stockpot, heat oil over medium-high heat. Add the next four ingredients; cook 6-8 minutes or until sausage is no longer pink and vegetables are tender. Add garlic; cook 1 minute.
2. Stir in Swiss chard, tomatoes, bay leaf and seasonings. Add broth; bring to a boil. Reduce heat; simmer, covered, 10-12 minutes or until Swiss chard is tender. Stir in beans and lemon juice; heat through. Remove bay leaf.

Nutrition Info:

- Info155 cal., 5g fat (1g sat. fat), 14mg chol., 658mg sod., 18g carb. (5g sugars, 5g fiber), 11g pro.

Chicken Tortilla Soup With Greens

Servings:8 | Cooking Time:7 Minutes

Ingredients:

- 8 (6-inch) corn tortillas, cut into ½-inch strips
- 2 tablespoons canola oil
- Salt
- 1½ pounds bone-in split chicken breasts, trimmed
- 12 ounces Swiss chard, stems chopped, leaves cut into 1-inch pieces
- 1 onion, chopped fine
- 1 tablespoon no-salt-added tomato paste
- 1–3 tablespoons minced canned chipotle chile in adobo sauce
- 1 (14.5-ounce) can no-salt-added diced tomatoes, drained
- 2 garlic cloves, minced
- 8 cups unsalted chicken broth
- 1 avocado, halved, pitted, and cut into ½-inch pieces
- 1 cup fresh cilantro leaves

Directions:

1. Adjust oven rack to middle position and heat oven to 425 degrees. Toss tortilla strips with 1 tablespoon oil and spread evenly onto rimmed baking sheet. Bake, stirring occasionally, until strips are deep golden brown and crisp, 8 to 12 minutes. Sprinkle tortillas with ¼ teaspoon salt and transfer to paper towel–lined plate.
2. Pat chicken dry with paper towels. Heat remaining 1 tablespoon oil in Dutch oven over medium-high heat until just smoking. Brown chicken, 3 to 5 minutes per side; transfer to plate and discard skin.
3. Add chard stems, onion, and ½ teaspoon salt to fat left in pot and cook until softened, about 5 minutes. Stir in tomato paste, chipotle plus sauce, and tomatoes and cook until mixture is dry and slightly darkened, 5 to 7 minutes. Stir in garlic and cook until fragrant, about 30 seconds.
4. Stir in broth, scraping up any browned bits. Nestle chicken into pot along with any accumulated juices and bring to simmer. Reduce heat to medium-low, cov-

er, and cook until chicken registers 160 degrees, 16 to 18 minutes. Transfer chicken to plate, let cool slightly, then shred into bite-size pieces using 2 forks.
5. Return soup to simmer, stir in chard leaves, and cook until mostly tender, about 5 minutes. Off heat, stir in chicken and let sit until heated through, about 5 minutes. Divide tortilla strips among individual serving bowls and ladle soup over top. Top with avocado and cilantro before serving.

Nutrition Info:

- Info270 cal., 10g fat (1g sag. fat), 60mg chol, 500mg sod., 19g carb (3g sugars, 5g fiber), 26g pro.

Cold-day Chicken Noodle Soup

Servings:8 | Cooking Time: 25 Minutes

Ingredients:

- 1 tablespoon canola oil
- 2 celery ribs, chopped
- 2 medium carrots, chopped
- 1 medium onion, chopped
- 8 cups reduced-sodium chicken broth
- 1/2 teaspoon dried basil
- 1/4 teaspoon pepper
- 3 cups uncooked whole wheat egg noodles (about 4 ounces)
- 3 cups coarsely chopped rotisserie chicken
- 1 tablespoon minced fresh parsley

Directions:

1. In a 6-qt. stockpot, heat oil over medium-high heat. Add celery, carrots and onion; cook and stir 5-7 minutes or until tender.
2. Add broth, basil and pepper; bring to a boil. Stir in the noodles; cook 12-14 minutes or until al dente. Stir in chicken and parsley; heat through.

Nutrition Info:

- Info195 cal., 6g fat (1g sat. fat), 47mg chol., 639mg sod., 16g carb. (2g sugars, 3g fiber), 21g pro.

Poultry Recipes

Recipe

....

From the kicthen of ....

Serves .... Prep time .... Cook time ....

☐ Difficulty   ☐ Easy   ☐ Medium   ☐ Hard

Ingredient

....

....

....

....

....

Directions ....

....

....

....

....

....

Poultry Recipes

Sausage-topped White Pizza

Servings:6 | Cooking Time: 30 Minutes

Ingredients:

- 2 hot Italian turkey sausage links, casings removed
- 1 cup reduced-fat ricotta cheese
- 1/4 teaspoon garlic powder
- 1 prebaked 12-inch thin whole wheat pizza crust
- 1 medium sweet red pepper, julienned
- 1 small onion, halved and thinly sliced
- 1/2 teaspoon Italian seasoning
- 1/4 teaspoon freshly ground pepper
- 1/4 teaspoon crushed red pepper flakes, optional
- 1/2 cup shredded part-skim mozzarella cheese
- 2 cups arugula or baby spinach

Directions:

1. Preheat oven to 450°. In a large skillet, cook and crumble sausage over medium-high heat until no longer pink, 4-6 minutes. Mix ricotta cheese and garlic powder.
2. Place crust on a baking sheet; spread with ricotta cheese mixture. Top with sausage, red pepper and onion; sprinkle with seasonings, then with the shredded mozzarella cheese.
3. Bake on a lower oven rack until edge is lightly browned and cheese is melted, 8-10 minutes. Top with arugula.

Nutrition Info:

- Info242 cal., 8g fat (4g sat. fat), 30mg chol., 504mg sod., 28g carb. (5g sugars, 4g fiber), 16g pro.

Spicy Barbecued Chicken

Servings:8 | Cooking Time: 30 Minutes

Ingredients:

- 1 tablespoon canola oil
- 2 garlic cloves, minced
- 1/2 cup chili sauce
- 3 tablespoons brown sugar
- 2 teaspoons salt-free seasoning blend, divided
- 3/4 teaspoon cayenne pepper, divided
- 2 teaspoons ground mustard
- 2 teaspoons chili powder
- 8 boneless skinless chicken breast halves (4 ounces each)

Directions:

1. In a small saucepan, heat oil over medium heat. Add garlic; cook and stir 1 minute. Add chili sauce, brown sugar, 1 teaspoon seasoning blend and 1/4 teaspoon cayenne. Bring to a boil; cook and stir for 1 minute. Remove from the heat.
2. In a small bowl, mix mustard, chili powder and remaining seasoning blend and cayenne; rub over chicken. Lightly coat grill rack with cooking oil.
3. Grill chicken, covered, over medium heat for 4 minutes. Turn; grill about 4-6 minutes longer or until a meat thermometer reads 165°, brushing chicken tops occasionally with the chili sauce mixture.

Nutrition Info:

- Info179 cal., 5g fat (1g sat. fat), 63mg chol., 293mg sod., 10g carb. (8g sugars, 0 fiber), 23g pro.

Citrus-spiced Roast Chicken

Servings:6 | Cooking Time: 1 Hour

Ingredients:

- 3 tablespoons orange marmalade
- 4 1/2 teaspoons chopped chipotle peppers in adobo sauce
- 3 garlic cloves, minced
- 3/4 teaspoon salt, divided
- 1/2 teaspoon ground cumin
- 1 broiler/fryer chicken (4 pounds)

Directions:

1. Preheat oven to 350°. Mix the marmalade, chipotle peppers, garlic, 1/2 teaspoon salt and cumin. With fingers, carefully loosen skin from chicken; rub mixture under the skin.
2. Place chicken on a rack in a shallow roasting pan, breast side up. Tuck wings under chicken; tie drumsticks together. Rub skin with remaining salt. Roast 1 to 1 1/4 hours or until a thermometer inserted in thickest part of thigh reads 170°-175°, covering chicken with foil halfway through cooking to prevent any overbrowning.
3. Remove chicken from the oven; let stand, loosely covered, for15 minutes before carving. Remove and discard the skin before serving.

Nutrition Info:

- Info239 cal., 8g fat (2g sat. fat), 98mg chol., 409mg sod., 8g carb. (6g sugars, 0 fiber), 32g pro.

Balsamic Chicken With Roasted Tomatoes

Servings:4 | Cooking Time: 25 Minutes

Ingredients:

- 2 tablespoons honey
- 2 tablespoons olive oil, divided
- 2 cups grape tomatoes
- 4 boneless skinless chicken breast halves (6 ounces each)
- 1/2 teaspoon salt
- 1/2 teaspoon pepper
- 2 tablespoons balsamic glaze

Directions:

1. Preheat oven to 400°. In a small bowl, mix honey and 1 tablespoon oil. Add the tomatoes and toss to coat. Transfer to a greased 15x10x1-in. baking pan. Bake 5-7 minutes or until softened.
2. Pound chicken breasts with a meat mallet to 1/2-in. thickness; sprinkle with salt and pepper. In a large skillet, heat remaining oil over medium heat. Add chicken; cook 5-6 minutes on each side or until no longer pink. Serve with the roasted tomatoes; drizzle with glaze.

Nutrition Info:

- Info306 cal., 11g fat (2g sat. fat), 94mg chol., 384mg sod., 16g carb. (14g sugars, 1g fiber), 35g pro.

Cool & Crunchy Chicken Salad

Servings:6 | Cooking Time: 25 Minutes

Ingredients:

- 1/2 cup reduced-fat mayonnaise
- 2 tablespoons minced fresh parsley
- 1 tablespoon lemon juice
- 1 tablespoon cider vinegar
- 1 teaspoon spicy brown mustard
- 1/2 teaspoon sugar
- 1/4 teaspoon salt
- 1/4 teaspoon pepper
- 3 cups cubed cooked chicken
- 1 cup seedless red grapes, halved
- 1 cup thinly sliced celery
- 1 cup pecan halves, toasted
- Lettuce leaves

Directions:

1. In a large bowl, mix the first eight ingredients until blended. Add chicken, grapes, celery and pecans; toss to coat. Serve on lettuce.

Nutrition Info:

- Info340 cal., 24g fat (3g sat. fat), 69mg chol., 311mg sod., 10g carb. (7g sugars, 2g fiber), 22g pro.

Slow Cooker Favorites

Recipe ....

From the kicthen of ....

Serves .... Prep time .... Cook time ....

☐ Difficulty   ☐ Easy   ☐ Medium   ☐ Hard

Ingredient   Yummy!

·   ·

·   ·

·   ·

·   ·

Directions ....

· ·

· ·

· ·

· ·

· ·

· ·

· ·

Slow Cooker Favorites

Braised Swiss Chard With Shiitakes And Peanuts

Servings:6 | Cooking Time: 2 Hours

Ingredients:

- 2 pounds Swiss chard, stems chopped fine, leaves cut into 1-inch pieces
- 4 ounces shiitake mushrooms, stemmed and sliced ¼ inch thick
- 3 garlic cloves, minced
- 2 teaspoons toasted sesame oil
- 2 teaspoons grated fresh ginger
- ⅛ teaspoon red pepper flakes
- 1 tablespoon rice vinegar
- Pepper
- ¼ cup chopped dry-roasted peanuts
- 2 scallions, sliced thin

Directions:

1. Lightly coat slow cooker with vegetable oil spray. Microwave chard stems, mushrooms, garlic, 1 teaspoon oil, 1 teaspoon ginger, and pepper flakes in bowl, stirring occasionally, until vegetables are softened, about 5 minutes; transfer to prepared slow cooker. Stir in chard leaves, cover, and cook until chard is tender, 1 to 2 hours on high.
2. Stir in vinegar, remaining 1 teaspoon oil, and remaining 1 teaspoon ginger. Season with pepper to taste. (Swiss chard can be held on warm or low setting for up to 2 hours.) Sprinkle with peanuts and scallions before serving.

Nutrition Info:

- Info90 cal., 5g fat (1g sag. fat), 0mg chol, 330mg sod., 9g carb (3g sugars, 3g fiber), 5g pro.

Chicken Thighs With Black-eyed Pea Ragout

Servings:6 | Cooking Time:7minutes

Ingredients:

- 1 pound kale, stemmed and chopped coarse
- 1 onion, chopped fine
- 4 garlic cloves, minced
- 1 tablespoon extra-virgin olive oil
- 1 teaspoon dry mustard
- 2 teaspoons minced fresh thyme or ½ teaspoon dried
- 2 (15-ounce) cans no-salt-added black-eyed peas, rinsed
- ½ cup unsalted chicken broth
- Salt and pepper
- 6 (5-ounce) bone-in chicken thighs, skin removed, trimmed of all visible fat
- 2 teaspoons hot sauce, plus extra for serving
- Lemon wedges

Directions:

1. Lightly coat oval slow cooker with vegetable oil spray. Microwave kale, onion, garlic, oil, mustard, and thyme in covered bowl, stirring occasionally, until vegetables are softened, 5 to 7 minutes; transfer to prepared slow cooker.
2. Process one-third of peas, broth, and ¼ teaspoon salt in food processor until smooth, about 30 seconds; transfer to slow cooker. Stir in remaining peas. Sprinkle chicken with ¼ teaspoon salt and ¼ teaspoon pepper and nestle into slow cooker. Cover and cook until chicken is tender, 4 to 5 hours on low.
3. Transfer chicken to serving platter. Stir hot sauce into ragout and season with pepper to taste. Serve chicken with ragout and lemon wedges, passing extra hot sauce separately.

Nutrition Info:

- Info240 cal., 8g fat (1g sag. fat), 80mg chol, 380mg sod., 20g carb (4g sugars, 6g fiber), 24g pro.

Teriyaki Beef Stew

Servings:8 | Cooking Time: 6 1/2 Hours

Ingredients:

- 2 pounds beef stew meat
- 1 bottle (12 ounces) ginger beer or ginger ale
- 1/4 cup teriyaki sauce
- 2 garlic cloves, minced
- 2 tablespoons sesame seeds
- 2 tablespoons cornstarch
- 2 tablespoons cold water
- 2 cups frozen peas, thawed
- Hot cooked rice, optional

Directions:

1. In a nonstick skillet, brown beef in batches. Transfer to a 3-qt. slow cooker.
2. In a small bowl, combine the ginger beer, teriyaki sauce, garlic and sesame seeds; pour over beef. Cover and cook on low for 6-8 hours or until the meat is tender.
3. Combine cornstarch and cold water until smooth; gradually stir into stew. Stir in peas. Cover and cook on high for 30 minutes or until thickened. Serve with rice if desired.

Nutrition Info:

- Info310 cal., 12g fat (4g sat. fat), 94mg chol., 528mg sod., 17g carb. (9g sugars, 2g fiber), 33g pro.

And Radishes

Servings:4 | Cooking Time: 2 Hours

Ingredients:

- 1½ pounds carrots, peeled and sliced ¼ inch thick on bias
- 10 radishes, trimmed and sliced ¼ inch thick
- ¼ cup unsalted chicken broth
- 3 tablespoons extra-virgin olive oil
- 1 teaspoon ground cumin
- 1 teaspoon paprika
- 1 (1-pound) pork tenderloin, trimmed of all visible fat
- Salt and pepper
- 2 tablespoons lime juice
- 2 tablespoons minced fresh cilantro
- 1 teaspoon minced canned chipotle chile in adobo sauce

Directions:

1. Microwave carrots and ¼ cup water in covered bowl, stirring occasionally, until crisp-tender, about 8 minutes. Drain carrots and transfer to oval slow cooker. Stir in radishes and broth.
2. Microwave 1 teaspoon oil, cumin, and paprika in bowl until fragrant, about 30 seconds; let cool slightly. Rub tenderloin with spice mixture and sprinkle with ¼ teaspoon salt and ⅛ teaspoon pepper. Nestle tenderloin into slow cooker, cover, and cook until pork registers 145 degrees, 1 to 2 hours on low.
3. Transfer tenderloin to carving board, tent with aluminum foil, and let rest for 5 minutes.
4. Whisk remaining 8 teaspoons oil, lime juice, cilantro, and chipotle together in bowl, then season dressing with pepper to taste. Drain vegetables from cooker and transfer to large bowl. Stir in 2 tablespoons of dressing and season with pepper to taste. Slice tenderloin ½ inch thick and serve with vegetables and remaining dressing.

Nutrition Info:

- Info300 cal., 14g fat (2g sag. fat), 75mg chol, 350mg sod., 20g carb (9g sugars, 6g fiber), 26g pro.

Carne Guisada

Servings:12 | Cooking Time: 7 Hours

Ingredients:

- 1 bottle (12 ounces) beer
- 1/4 cup all-purpose flour
- 2 tablespoons tomato paste
- 1 jalapeno pepper, seeded and chopped
- 4 teaspoons Worcestershire sauce
- 1 bay leaf
- 2 to 3 teaspoons crushed red pepper flakes
- 2 teaspoons chili powder
- 1 1/2 teaspoons ground cumin
- 1/2 teaspoon salt
- 1/2 teaspoon paprika
- 2 garlic cloves, minced
- 1/2 teaspoon red wine vinegar
- Dash liquid smoke, optional
- 1 boneless pork shoulder butt roast (3 pounds), cut into 2-inch pieces
- 2 large unpeeled red potatoes, chopped
- 1 medium onion, chopped
- Whole wheat tortillas or hot cooked brown rice, lime wedges and chopped fresh cilantro, optional

Directions:

1. In a 4- or 5-qt. slow cooker, mix first 13 ingredients and, if desired, the liquid smoke. Stir in pork, potatoes and onion. Cook mixture, covered, on low until pork is tender, 7-9 hours.
2. Discard bay leaf; skim fat from cooking juices. Shred pork slightly with two forks. Serve pork with the optional remaining ingredients as desired.

Nutrition Info:

- Info261 cal., 12g fat (4g sat. fat), 67mg chol., 200mg sod., 16g carb. (3g sugars, 2g fiber), 21g pro.

Spiced Pork Tenderloin With Carrots Slow Cooker Beef Tostadas

Servings:6 | Cooking Time: 6 Hours

Ingredients:

- 1 large onion, chopped
- 1/4 cup lime juice
- 1 jalapeno pepper, seeded and minced
- 1 serrano pepper, seeded and minced
- 1 tablespoon chili powder
- 3 garlic cloves, minced
- 1/2 teaspoon ground cumin
- 1 beef top round steak (about 1 1/2 pounds)
- 1 teaspoon salt
- 1/2 teaspoon pepper
- 1/4 cup chopped fresh cilantro
- 12 corn tortillas (6 inches)
- Cooking spray
- TOPPINGS
- 1 1/2 cups shredded lettuce
- 1 medium tomato, finely chopped
- 3/4 cup shredded sharp cheddar cheese
- 3/4 cup reduced-fat sour cream, optional

Directions:

1. Place the first seven ingredients in a 3- or 4-qt. slow cooker. Cut steak in half and sprinkle with salt and pepper; add to slow cooker. Cook, covered, on low 6-8 hours or until meat is tender.
2. Remove meat; cool slightly. Shred meat with two forks. Return beef to slow cooker and stir in cilantro; heat through. Spritz both sides of tortillas with cooking spray. Place in a single layer on baking sheets; broil 1-2 minutes on each side or until crisp. Spoon the beef mixture over the tortillas; top with lettuce, tomato, cheese and, if desired, sour cream.

Nutrition Info:

- Info372 cal., 13g fat (6g sat. fat), 88mg chol., 602mg sod., 30g carb. (5g sugars, 5g fiber), 35g pro.

Special Treats

RECIPES

DATE

RECIPES		Salads	Meats	Soups
SERVES		Grains	Seafood	Snack
PREP TIME		Breads	Vegetables	Breakfast
COOK TIME		Appetizers	Desserts	Lunch
FROM THE KITCHEN OF		Main Dishes	Beverages	Dinners

INGREDIENTS

DIRECTIONS

NOTES

SERVING	☆☆☆☆☆
DIFFICULTY	☆☆☆☆☆
OVERALL	☆☆☆☆☆

Special Treats

Fig Bars

Servings:16 | Cooking Time:45 Minutes

Ingredients:

- 1 cup (5 ounces) all-purpose flour
- 2 teaspoons ground allspice
- ½ teaspoon salt
- ¼ teaspoon baking powder
- 8 tablespoons unsalted butter, cut into ½-inch pieces and chilled
- ½ cup plus 3 tablespoons no-sugar-added apple juice
- 1 cup dried Turkish or Calimyrna figs, stemmed and quartered
- ¼ cup sliced almonds, toasted
- ¼ cup shelled pistachios, toasted and chopped

Directions:

1. Adjust oven rack to middle position and heat oven to 375 degrees. Make foil sling for 8-inch square baking pan by folding 2 long sheets of aluminum foil so each is 8 inches wide. Lay sheets of foil in pan perpendicular to each other, with extra foil hanging over edges of pan. Push foil into corners and up sides of pan, smoothing foil flush to pan. Grease foil.

2. Pulse flour, allspice, salt, and baking powder in food processor until combined, about 3 pulses. Scatter chilled butter over top and pulse until mixture resembles wet sand, about 10 pulses. Add 3 tablespoons apple juice and pulse until dough comes together, about 8 pulses.

3. Transfer mixture to prepared pan and press into even layer with bottom of dry measuring cup. Bake crust until golden brown, 35 to 40 minutes, rotating pan halfway through baking. Let crust cool completely in pan, about 45 minutes.

4. Microwave figs and remaining ½ cup apple juice in covered bowl until slightly softened, about 2 minutes. Puree fig mixture in now-empty food processor until smooth, about 15 seconds. Spread fig mixture evenly over cooled crust, then sprinkle with almonds and pistachios, pressing to adhere. Using foil overhang, lift bars from pan and transfer to cutting board. Cut into 16 squares and serve.

Nutrition Info:

- Info130 cal., 7g fat (3g sag. fat), 15mg chol, 80mg sod., 15g carb (6g sugars, 2g fiber), 2g pro.

Saucy Spiced Pears

Servings:4 | Cooking Time: 20 Minutes

Ingredients:

- 1/2 cup orange juice
- 2 tablespoons butter
- 2 tablespoons sugar
- 2 teaspoons lemon juice
- 1 teaspoon vanilla extract
- 1 teaspoon ground ginger
- 1/4 teaspoon ground cinnamon
- 1/8 teaspoon salt
- 1/8 teaspoon ground allspice
- 1/8 teaspoon cayenne pepper, optional
- 3 large Bosc pears (about 1 3/4 pounds), cored, peeled and sliced
- Thinly sliced fresh mint leaves, optional

Directions:

1. In a large skillet, combine the first nine ingredients and, if desired, cayenne. Cook over medium-high heat 1-2 minutes or until butter is melted, stirring occasionally.

2. Add pears; bring to a boil. Reduce heat to medium; cook, uncovered, 3-4 minutes or until sauce is slightly thickened and pears are crisp-tender, stirring occasionally. Cool slightly. If desired, top with mint.

Nutrition Info:

- Info192 cal., 6g fat (4g sat. fat), 15mg chol., 130mg sod., 36g carb. (26g sugars, 5g fiber), 1g pro.

Frozen Yogurt Fruit Pops

Servings:1 | Cooking Time: 15 Minutes

Ingredients:

- 2 1/4 cups (18 ounces) raspberry yogurt
- 2 tablespoons lemon juice
- 2 medium ripe bananas, cut into chunks
- 12 freezer pop molds or 12 paper cups (3 ounces each) and wooden pop sticks

Directions:

1. Place the yogurt, lemon juice and bananas in a blender; cover and process until smooth, stopping to stir mixture if necessary.
2. Pour mixture into molds or paper cups. Top molds with holders. If using cups, top with foil and insert sticks through foil. Freeze until firm.

Nutrition Info:

- Info60 cal., 1g fat (0 sat. fat), 2mg chol., 23mg sod., 13g carb. (10g sugars, 1g fiber), 2g pro.

Peaches, Blackberries, And Strawberries With Basil And Pepper

Servings:6 | Cooking Time:15 Minutes

Ingredients:

- Nectarines can be substituted for the peaches.
- 2 teaspoons sugar
- 2 tablespoons chopped fresh basil
- ½ teaspoon pepper
- 3 peaches, halved, pitted, and cut into ½-inch pieces
- 10 ounces (2 cups) blackberries
- 10 ounces strawberries, hulled and quartered (2 cups)
- 1 tablespoon lime juice, plus extra for seasoning

Directions:

1. Combine sugar, basil, and pepper in large bowl. Using rubber spatula, press mixture into side of bowl until sugar becomes damp, about 30 seconds. Add peaches, blackberries, and strawberries and gently toss to combine. Let sit at room temperature, stirring occasionally, until fruit releases its juices, 15 to 30 minutes. Stir in lime juice and season with extra lime juice to taste. Serve.

Nutrition Info:

- Info70 cal., 0g fat (0g sag. fat), 0mg chol, 0mg sod., 18g carb (13g sugars, 5g fiber), 2g pro.

No-fuss Banana Ice Cream

Servings:1 | Cooking Time: 15 Minutes

Ingredients:

- 6 very ripe bananas
- ½ cup heavy cream
- 1 tablespoon vanilla extract
- 1 teaspoon lemon juice
- ¼ teaspoon salt
- ¼ teaspoon ground cinnamon

Directions:

1. Peel bananas, place in large zipper-lock bag, and press out excess air. Freeze bananas until solid, at least 8 hours.
2. Let bananas sit at room temperature to soften slightly, about 15 minutes. Slice into ½-inch-thick rounds and place in food processor. Add cream, vanilla, lemon juice, salt, and cinnamon and process until smooth, about 5 minutes, scraping down sides of bowl as needed.
3. Transfer mixture to airtight container and freeze until firm, at least 2 hours or up to 5 days. Serve.

Nutrition Info:

- Info160 cal., 6g fat (3g sag. fat), 15mg chol, 75mg sod., 28g carb (18g sugars, 3g fiber), 1g pro.

Nectarines And Berries In Prosecco

Servings:8 | Cooking Time:15 Minutes

Ingredients:

- 10 ounces (2 cups) blackberries or raspberries
- 10 ounces strawberries, hulled and quartered (2 cups)
- 1 pound nectarines, pitted and cut into ¼-inch wedges
- 1 tablespoon sugar
- 1 tablespoon orange liqueur, such as Grand Marnier or triple sec
- 2 tablespoons chopped fresh mint
- ¼ teaspoon grated lemon zest
- ¾ cup chilled prosecco

Directions:

1. Gently toss blackberries, strawberries, nectarines, sugar, orange liqueur, mint, and lemon zest together in large bowl. Let sit at room temperature, stirring occasionally, until fruit begins to release its juices, about 15 minutes. Just before serving, pour prosecco over fruit.

Nutrition Info:

- Info80 cal., 0g fat (0g sag. fat), 0mg chol, 0mg sod., 14g carb (10g sugars, 3g fiber), 1g pro.

Strawberry Pot Stickers

Servings:32 | Cooking Time: 10 Minutes

Ingredients:

- 3 ounces milk chocolate, chopped
- 1/4 cup half-and-half cream
- 1 teaspoon butter
- 1 teaspoon vanilla extract
- 1/4 teaspoon ground cinnamon
- POT STICKERS
- 2 cups chopped fresh strawberries
- 3 ounces milk chocolate, chopped
- 1 tablespoon brown sugar
- 1/4 teaspoon ground cinnamon
- 32 pot sticker or gyoza wrappers
- 1 large egg, lightly beaten
- 2 tablespoons canola oil, divided
- 1/2 cup water, divided

Directions:

1. Place chocolate in a small bowl. In a small saucepan, bring cream and butter just to a boil. Pour over chocolate; whisk until smooth. Stir in vanilla and cinnamon. Cool to room temperature, stirring occasionally.

2. For pot stickers, in a small bowl, toss strawberries and chopped chocolate with brown sugar and cinnamon. Place 1 tablespoon mixture in center of 1 gyoza wrapper. (Cover remaining wrappers with a damp paper towel until ready to use.)

3. Moisten wrapper edge with egg. Fold wrapper over filling; seal edges, pleating the front side several times to form a pleated pouch. Repeat with remaining wrappers and filling. Stand pot stickers on a work surface to flatten bottoms; curve slightly to form crescent shapes, if desired.

4. In a large skillet, heat 1 tablespoon oil over medium-high heat. Arrange half of the pot stickers, flat side down, in concentric circles in pan; cook 1-2 minutes or until bottoms are golden brown. Add 1/4 cup water; bring to a simmer. Cook, covered, 3-5 minutes or until water is almost absorbed and wrappers are tender.

5. Cook, uncovered, 1 minute or until bottoms are crisp and the water is completely evaporated. Repeat with remaining pot stickers. Serve the pot stickers with chocolate sauce.

Nutrition Info:

- Info58 cal., 3g fat (1g sat. fat), 6mg chol., 18mg sod., 8g carb. (4g sugars, 0 fiber), 1g pro.

Vegetables, Fruit And Side Dishes

Recipe

....

From the kicthen of ....

Serves .... Prep time .... Cook time ....

☐ Difficulty   ☐ Easy   ☐ Medium   ☐ Hard

Ingredient

....

....

....

....

....

Directions ....

....

....

....

....

....

....

Vegetables, Fruit And Side Dishes

Squash Melt

Servings: 4 | Cooking Time: 8 Minutes

Ingredients:

- 2 medium yellow squash (about 12 ounces total), cut in 1/8-inch rounds
- 1 medium green bell pepper, chopped or 1 cup thinly sliced yellow onion
- 1/4–1/2 teaspoon dried oregano
- 1/4 teaspoon salt
- 1/4 cup shredded, reduced-fat, sharp cheddar cheese

Directions:

1. Place a medium nonstick skillet over medium-high heat until hot. Coat the skillet with nonstick cooking spray and add all the ingredients except the cheese.
2. Coat the vegetables with nonstick cooking spray and cook 6–7 minutes or until the vegetables are tender, stirring constantly. Use two utensils to stir as you would when stir-frying.
3. Remove the skillet from the heat and sprinkle the vegetables evenly with the cheese. Cover and let stand 2 minutes to melt the cheese.

Nutrition Info:

- Info40 cal., 1g fat (0g sag. fat), 5mg chol, 190mg sod., 5g carb (3g sugars, 2g fiber), 3g pro.

Smoky Cauliflower

Servings: 8 | Cooking Time: 30 Minutes

Ingredients:

- 1 large head cauliflower, broken into 1-inch florets (about 9 cups)
- 2 tablespoons olive oil
- 1 teaspoon smoked paprika
- 3/4 teaspoon salt
- 2 garlic cloves, minced
- 2 tablespoons minced fresh parsley

Directions:

1. Place cauliflower florets in a large bowl. Combine the oil, paprika and salt. Drizzle over cauliflower; toss to coat. Transfer to a 15x10x1-in. baking pan. Bake, uncovered, at 450° for about 10 minutes.
2. Stir in garlic. Bake 10-15 minutes longer or until cauliflower is tender and lightly browned, stirring occasionally. Sprinkle with parsley.

Nutrition Info:

- Info58 cal., 4g fat (0 sat. fat), 0 chol., 254mg sod., 6g carb. (3g sugars, 3g fiber), 2g pro.

Fresh Lemon Roasted Brussels Sprouts

Servings: 4 | Cooking Time: 20 Minutes

Ingredients:

- 1 pound fresh Brussels sprouts, ends trimmed and halved
- 2 tablespoons extra-virgin olive oil, divided
- Juice and zest of 1 medium lemon
- 2 teaspoons Worcestershire sauce
- 1/4 teaspoon pepper

Directions:

1. Preheat oven 425°F.
2. Toss Brussels sprouts with 1 tablespoon oil, place in a single layer on a foil-lined baking sheet. Roast 10 minutes, stir, and cook 10 minutes or until just tender and beginning to brown.
3. Remove, toss with remaining ingredients and 1/4 teaspoon salt, if desired.

Nutrition Info:

- Info115 cal., 7g fat (1g sag. fat), 0mg chol, 55mg sod., 13g carb (3g sugars, 5g fiber), 4g pro.

Roasted Beans And Green Onions

Servings: 4 | Cooking Time:11 Minutes

Ingredients:

- 8 ounces green string beans, trimmed
- 4 whole green onions, trimmed and cut in fourths (about 3-inch pieces)
- 1 1/2 teaspoons extra virgin olive oil
- 1/4 teaspoon salt

Directions:

1. Preheat the oven to 425°F.
2. Line a baking sheet with foil and coat the foil with nonstick cooking spray.
3. Toss the beans, onions, and oil together in a medium bowl. Arrange them in a thin layer on the baking sheet.
4. Bake for 8 minutes and stir gently, using two utensils as you would for a stir-fry. Bake another 3–4 minutes or until the beans begin to brown on the edges and are tender-crisp.
5. Remove the pan from the oven and sprinkle the beans with salt.

Nutrition Info:

- Info35 cal., 2g fat (0g sag. fat), 0mg chol, 150mg sod., 5g carb (1g sugars, 2g fiber), 1g pro.

Parmesan Butternut Squash

Servings:8 | Cooking Time: 25 Minutes

Ingredients:

- 1 medium butternut squash (about 3 pounds), peeled and cut into 1-inch cubes
- 2 tablespoons water
- 1/2 cup panko (Japanese) bread crumbs
- 1/2 cup grated Parmesan cheese
- 1/4 teaspoon salt
- 1/8 teaspoon pepper

Directions:

1. Place squash and water in a large microwave-safe bowl. Microwave, covered, on high 15-17 minutes or until tender; drain.
2. Preheat broiler. Transfer squash to a greased 15x10x1-in. baking pan. Toss bread crumbs with cheese, salt and pepper; sprinkle over squash. Broil 3-4 in. from heat 1-2 minutes or until topping is golden brown.

Nutrition Info:

- Info112 cal., 2g fat (1g sat. fat), 4mg chol., 168mg sod., 23g carb. (5g sugars, 6g fiber), 4g pro.

Confetti Corn

Servings:4 | Cooking Time: 15 Minutes

Ingredients:

- 1/4 cup chopped carrot
- 1 tablespoon olive oil
- 2 3/4 cups fresh or frozen corn, thawed
- 1/4 cup chopped water chestnuts
- 1/4 cup chopped sweet red pepper

Directions:

1. In a large skillet, saute the carrot in oil until crisp-tender. Stir in the corn, water chestnuts and red pepper; heat until warmed through.

Nutrition Info:

- Info140 cal., 4g fat (1g sat. fat), 0 chol., 7mg sod., 26g carb. (3g sugars, 3g fiber), 4g pro.

Sautéed Zucchini Ribbons

Servings:6 | Cooking Time:18 Minutes

Ingredients:

- 1 small garlic clove, minced
- 1 teaspoon grated lemon zest plus 1 tablespoon juice
- 4 (6- to 8-ounce) zucchini and/or yellow summer squash, trimmed
- 2 tablespoons plus 1 teaspoon extra-virgin olive oil
- Salt and pepper
- 1½ tablespoons chopped fresh parsley

Directions:

1. Combine garlic and lemon juice in large bowl and set aside for at least 10 minutes. Using vegetable peeler, shave off 3 ribbons from 1 side of summer squash, then turn squash 90 degrees and shave off 3 more ribbons. Continue to turn and shave ribbons until you reach seeds; discard core. Repeat with remaining squash.
2. Whisk 2 tablespoons oil, ¼ teaspoon salt, ⅛ teaspoon pepper, and lemon zest into garlic–lemon juice mixture.
3. Heat remaining 1 teaspoon oil in 12-inch nonstick skillet over medium-high heat until just smoking. Add squash and cook, tossing occasionally with tongs, until squash has softened and is translucent, 3 to 4 minutes. Transfer squash to bowl with dressing, add parsley, and gently toss to coat. Season with pepper to taste. Serve.

Nutrition Info:

- Info70 cal., 6g fat (1g sag. fat), 0mg chol, 105mg sod., 4g carb (2g sugars, 1g fiber), 1g pro.

Hot Skillet Pineapple

Servings: 4 | Cooking Time:7 Minutes

Ingredients:

- 2 tablespoons no-trans-fat margarine (35% vegetable oil)
- 1 1/2 teaspoons packed dark brown sugar
- 1/2 teaspoon ground curry powder
- 8 slices pineapple packed in juice

Directions:

1. Place a large nonstick skillet over medium-high heat until hot. Add the margarine, sugar, and curry and bring to a boil. Stir to blend.
2. Arrange the pineapple slices in a single layer in the skillet. Cook 6 minutes until the pineapples are richly golden in color, turning frequently.
3. Arrange the pineapples on a serving platter and let stand 5 minutes to develop flavors and cool slightly. Serve hot or room temperature.

Nutrition Info:

- Info70 cal., 2g fat (0g sag. fat), 0mg chol, 45mg sod., 13g carb (12g sugars, 1g fiber), 0g pro.

Appendix : Recipes Index

A

Apple Spiced Tea 16

Asian Marinated Mushrooms 23

Avocado & Garbanzo Bean Quinoa Salad 36

And Radishes 60

B

Balsamic-goat Cheese Grilled Plums 23

Brown Rice With Tomatoes And Chickpeas 33

Black Beans With Bell Peppers & Rice 38

Balsamic Chicken With Roasted Tomatoes 56

Braised Swiss Chard With Shiitakes And Peanuts 59

C

Calico Scrambled Eggs 17

Cheesy Snack Mix 21

Crostini With Kalamata Tomato 22

Crunchy Tuna Wraps 26

Cheesy Shrimp And Grits 27

Creamy Chipotle Chile Sauce 28

Chickpeas With Garlic And Parsley 31

Cumin'd Salsa Salad 41

Chunky Veggie Slaw 42

Chinese Starter Soup 50

Creamy Butternut Soup 50

Chicken Tortilla Soup With Greens 52

Cold-day Chicken Noodle Soup 52

Citrus-spiced Roast Chicken 56

Cool & Crunchy Chicken Salad 56

Chicken Thighs With Black-eyed Pea Ragout 59

Carne Guisada 61

Confetti Corn 70

E

Edamame Corn Carrot Salad 41

F

Fresh Fruit Combo 16

Fantastic Fish Tacos 27

Fig Bars 64

Frozen Yogurt Fruit Pops 65

Fresh Lemon Roasted Brussels Sprouts 69

G

Guacamole 18

Garden-fresh Wraps 22

Gazpacho Salad 42

Greek-style Ravioli 45

Garlic Pork Roast 46

H

Hearty Vegetable Lentil Soup 51

Hot Skillet Pineapple 71

I

Italian Veggie Beef Soup 50

L

Lime'd Blueberries 21

Light Parmesan Pasta 36

Lemony Asparagus Spear Salad 42

M

Mixed Fruit With Lemon-basil Dressing 17

Maple Apple Baked Oatmeal 18

Mango Avocado Spring Rolls 23

N

No-fuss Banana Ice Cream 65

Nectarines And Berries In Prosecco 66

O

Open-faced Roast Beef Sandwiches 45

One-pot Beef & Pepper Stew 47

P

Pickled Shrimp With Basil 21

Parmesan Potato Bake 33

Peaches, Blackberries, And Strawberries With Basil And Pepper 65

Parmesan Butternut Squash 70

R

Raspberry Peach Puff Pancake 16

Ricotta-stuffed Portobello Mushrooms 37

Roasted Beans And Green Onions 70

S

Seared Scallops With Snap Pea And Edamame Slaw 28

Sicilian White Beans And Escarole 31

Skillet-grilled Meatless Burgers With Spicy Sour Cream 38

Smoky Sirloin 46

Sassy Salsa Meat Loaves 47

Sausage & Greens Soup 51

Sausage-topped White Pizza 55

Spicy Barbecued Chicken 55

Spiced Pork Tenderloin With Carrots Slow Cooker Beef Tostadas 61

Saucy Spiced Pears 64

Strawberry Pot Stickers 66

Smoky Cauliflower 69

Squash Melt 69

Sautéed Zucchini Ribbons 71

T

Tomato-jalapeno Granita 22

Tomato-poached Halibut 26

Tomato Topper Over Anything 36

Tasty Lentil Tacos 37

Teriyaki Beef Stew 60

W

Warm Farro With Mushrooms And Thyme 32

Wheat Berry Salad With Roasted Red Pepper, Feta, And Arugula 32

Warm Spinach Salad With Feta And Pistachios 41

Weeknight Pasta 45

Printed in Great Britain
by Amazon